Celebrating
Advent

Celebrating Advent

Family Devotions and Activities
for the Christmas Season

ANN HIBBARD

Revell
a division of Baker Publishing Group
Grand Rapids, Michigan

Published by Revell
a division of Baker Publishing Group
P.O. Box 6287, Grand Rapids, MI 49516-6287
www.revellbooks.com

New paperback edition published 2011

Previously published by Baker Books in 1993 under the title *Family Celebrations at Christmas*

Printed in the United States of America

Library of Congress Cataloging-in-Publication Data
Hibbard, Ann, 1956–
    Celebrating Advent : family devotions and activities for the Christmas season
/ Ann Hibbard.
        p. cm.
    Includes index.
    ISBN: 978-0-8007-2064-3 (pbk.)
    1. Advent—Prayers and devotions. 2. Christmas—Prayers and devotions.
3. Families—Prayers and devotions. I. Title.
BV40.H529 2011
242'.33—dc23   2011020362

11   12   13   14   15   16   17   7   6   5   4   3   2   1

Contents

Part 1

A Fresh Approach to the Holidays

1

What's Missing at Christmas?

What a relief! I thought as I finished addressing the last parcel wrapped in brown grocery bag paper. Our dining room looked as though a tornado had struck. Wrapping paper, grocery bags, scissors, tape, and old gift boxes were strewn everywhere. Fortunately, both kids were down for naps (a true miracle!), so I had been able to finish my Christmas wrapping without worrying about little fingers.

Turning my back on the mess, I retreated to the kitchen to put on the teakettle. I deserved a reward—a nice hot cup of Swiss Mocha.

"I hope everyone likes what we got them," I said to myself. I had certainly worked hard enough at it, trying to find gifts that people didn't already have, that suited their interests or their style, and that didn't overreach our limited budget. My stomach twisted into knots at the thought of all the money I had spent—yet I had been as frugal as possible, I silently argued.

Slowly I carried my steaming mug into the living room and curled up on the sofa across from the Christmas tree. The colorful lights pierced the winter gloom that was already creeping into the late afternoon. The lights seemed to pierce my heart as well with a stab of conflicting emotions. The little girl within me wanted to dance with excitement. Yet the mother that I had become felt depleted and depressed.

Why does Christmas have to be so much work? I thought bitterly. Beginning in October, Christmas was the focus of much of my thoughts, time, and energy—planning, shopping, mailing Christmas cards, scheduling, baking, decorating, more shopping, and wrapping. And I was exhausted by all the Christmas programs, activities, and social obligations. By the time Christmas arrived, I was too worn out to enjoy it.

Suddenly I realized that I had come to dread Christmas and all it entailed.

"Where *is* Christ in all of this?" I wondered.

The pressures of our cultural Christmas celebrations crowd in on us. We find ourselves running in a million different directions. "O little town of Bethlehem, how still we see thee lie" sounds like mockery as it comes over the sound system at the shopping mall.

Where *is* Christ in all of this?

Christian families feel the tension more acutely than any. Christmas should be a joyous celebration of our Lord's birth. We want our children to grow up with treasured memories of family times at Christmas—times when Christ is honored in our family.

This is what we long for, but somehow we don't know how to make it happen.

I have good news for you! You *can* make your family Christmas celebration a new and wonderful experience. Your family *can* meet Christ in a fresh way this Christmas season. Your children *can* get excited about celebrating Christ's coming.

The secret lies in this very simple exercise: bring Christ into the season of preparation. Spend a brief time together as a family each evening (or morning) focusing on the coming of Christ. You will find, as I and many others have found, that this transforms your Christmas.

"But I couldn't begin to come up with such a plan!" you protest. "I'm not that creative—and it sounds like too much work!"

Relax. The work has been done for you. *Celebrating Advent* will guide your family step by step through Advent and Christmas with fun and meaningful devotions for the entire family. You will find instructions and patterns for several projects which will enhance the devotional times while reinforcing the Scripture passages. Because music is such an important element of family times at Christmas, a selection of Christmas and Advent hymns is included, both words and music. Finally, you will glean practical ideas for relieving the stress and recapturing the peace and joy of the season.

Do you deeply desire to place Jesus Christ at the heart of your family celebrations? It is my prayer that *Celebrating Advent* will help you in that glorious endeavor.

Steps to a Happier Christmas

Most people fondly dream of a "Currier and Ives" Christmas, complete with blazing fires and Christmas carols sung around a tinsel-draped tree with a loving, harmonious family. For many, however, Christmas serves as a stark reminder of family tensions, grief, and broken relationships. Christmas cheer gives way to dashed hopes and holiday depression.

Many of us simply dread Christmas because of all the work. How in the world can we fit Christmas card-writing, baking, and endless hours of shopping into already packed schedules?

Why can't Christmas be the season of peace and joy that we crave? No matter what your situation, there is hope. This Christmas can be the most meaningful Christmas of your life.

Here are some practical steps which have helped me to change the tone of my Christmas.

Step One—Adopt Realistic Expectations

My mother's Swedish heritage played a big part in how we celebrated Christmas. Much time was devoted to baking a dozen different kinds of traditional Christmas cookies, which we then stored in the basement freezer. When anyone stopped by, we ran to the basement with a plate and filled it up with mouth-watering cookies. This is a sacred ritual in homes of Scandinavian descent.

When I married and moved away, I felt the necessity of carrying on the tradition. Many of the traditional cookies were not favorites of my husband. Without a big freezer in the basement, I had no place to keep the cookies fresh. I ended up with dozens of stale cookies, representing hours of labor. When children arrived, the Christmas baking seemed an insurmountable task.

Most of the pressure we feel at Christmas can be attributed to expectations—preconceived ideas of what Christmas should be. These pressures come from our culture, from our family members, and from within ourselves.

Where (and with whom) will we celebrate Christmas? For whom do we buy gifts? How much do we spend? What about Santa Claus? What kind of tree? What do we eat on Christmas Eve or Christmas Day? We all have differing expectations based on previous experience and current convictions.

As if this weren't bad enough, often our own expectations and those forced on us by others don't match. Those of us who like to "please everyone" find ourselves squeezed in an emotional vise. It is simply impossible to make everyone happy—nor should this be our goal.

Admit Our Limitations

In order to free ourselves from the bondage of all these expectations, we first need to admit that we cannot do it all. We simply cannot be everything to everyone. We need to take a good look at our own limitations. Each of us has limited time, energy, abilities, and resources. Because we are finite, we need to make choices— what we will and will not do. I needed to admit that making twelve kinds of Christmas cookies was no longer a priority for me.

Agree on a Realistic Plan

Once we admit our limitations, we need to agree on a realistic plan for Christmas. This means sitting down with your family, particularly your spouse if you are married, and discussing your hopes for your Christmas season.

If your children are old enough, include them in the discussion. Find out what is important to each person in terms of celebrating Christmas. What traditions does each one cherish? What activities are important for the family to attend? Have your calendar handy so that you can mark out the times and dates to do those special things.

Don't forget to leave time for quiet family evenings at home. One of our favorite family activities at Christmas is to build a fire in the fireplace and snuggle up together in front of the fire with the Christmas tree lights shining and favorite Christmas carols playing on the stereo.

Accept What We Cannot Change

We need to accept the "givens" of our situation. My friend Rita's husband left her three years ago. For Rita, Christmas is one of the most difficult times of the year. She can't help but remember happier times when she and Steve and the kids were one united family. Now she and Steve must split time with the children during holidays. She is no longer invited to parties that she and Steve went to as a couple. Worst of all, the children are hurt and confused, and Rita carries their pain as well as her own.

As much as Rita hates her situation, she has had to accept it. It only makes things worse to complain and to feel sorry for herself. She grieves this tremendous loss, but she has had to accept the reality of the situation and move ahead. At Christmas, this means finding new ways to make the season special, fun, and meaningful for her children and for herself.

Ask yourself, *does the success of my Christmas depend on someone else's behavior?* Often family dynamics at holidays are like a pressure cooker ready to explode. Chances are, people will behave badly. The patterns that our relationships fall into normally are just as prevalent at Christmas—if not more so.

Remember: You are not responsible for others' behavior— only your own. If you can realistically accept the givens in your situation, you will be less anxious and more at liberty to make a positive difference.

Step Two—Put Aside Resentment

The second step to a happier Christmas is to put aside resentment. Underlying anger saps our energy and chokes our joy.

My friend Sandy confessed to me, "I just dread another Christmas with my parents. My mom is so critical of me. Nothing I do meets with her approval. She still treats me like a child, and what's worse, when I'm around her, I act like one!"

Sandy had to make a choice. Either she could spend Christmas looking for fuel to stoke the fire of her bitterness, or she could let her mother's hurtful remarks slide by and instead concentrate on doing what she could to make Christmas special. Eventually, Sandy sought wise Christian counsel in dealing with her relationship with her parents, and God transformed those relationships. It is important to deal with underlying tensions and conflicts in family relationships. A family gathering at Christmas is not the best setting to tackle these issues, however.

If that person who continues to hurt or annoy you never changes, what will you do? Holding on to resentment turns us into bitter, negative people. I for one do not want to turn into such a person. But is there an alternative?

Someone has said that "To forgive is to set the prisoner free, only to discover that the prisoner was you."

Christmas is a wonderful time to begin to forgive those who have hurt or disappointed you. After all, the reason Jesus Christ came to earth was to bring forgiveness for our sins and restoration to our broken relationship with God. And he will give us the power to forgive others if we have given our lives to him and are seeking to love and obey him.

Step Three—Change What You Can

In working through the intricacies of her relationship with her mother, my friend Sandy finally realized that nothing she could do or say would change the way her mother acted. The only things Sandy could change, the only things over which she had any control, were her own attitudes and actions. Once

Sandy's attitudes and actions were coming from a more Christ-like perspective, the entire dynamic of her relationship with her mother changed for the better and both she and her mom were happier.

Once you have accepted the reality of your situation and put aside any resentment, you need to determine what you can do to make your Christmas better. Here are some suggestions for relieving the pressure so that you can be at your best.

Physical

When Elijah was exhausted after his showdown with the prophets of Baal on Mt. Carmel, he became depressed to the point of wanting to die. God sent his angel to minister to Elijah in the desert, and the first order of business was food and rest (see 1 Kings 19). Physical depletion quickly translates into emotional and spiritual depression. In order to be at our best for the Christmas season, we need to take care of ourselves physically. Getting enough sleep should be a priority. Rest does wonders for a person's temper as well as one's perspective.

I have found that regular exercise is a tremendous boost to my overall well-being. I try to walk two or three miles at least four times a week. Often I use that time to pray or to think through my schedule or my relationships. Invariably I return refreshed, energized, and with a new perspective.

Emotional

PLAN A SANE SCHEDULE

Essential to maintaining emotional equilibrium during the Christmas season is to plan a sane schedule. Write out a list of the things that you need to do, then get your calendar and plan when you will do them. Often tasks don't seem quite so daunting when they are broken down into bite-sized pieces.

I must confess that I am easily overwhelmed by a busy schedule. If I have one obligation on my calendar per day for a week, I experience a panic attack! Most people can handle more activities than I can. You need to know your own threshold and the kind of pace that your family can handle comfortably.

Allow me to put in one word of caution here, however: If we are always on the run, we miss hearing some important voices. We can miss hearing our children's voices—they see that we are too busy, so they don't share what is troubling them. We can miss hearing our spouse's voice, for we never have a chance to talk. Most importantly, we miss hearing God's voice. Slow down enough so that you can hear these voices this Christmas.

CONFIDE IN A FRIEND

I also find greater emotional strength as I confide in a friend. I have a handful of dear friends upon whom I depend for support, prayer, and wise counsel. Several of these friendships go back twelve to fourteen years. We have seen each other through many life changes. These friends know me well, and we have helped one another grow closer to the Lord. Several friendships have emerged in the past year or two. God is using these new relationships to cause me to grow in new areas. When I am troubled or anxious, I turn to one of these friends for prayer. Such a friendship is a priceless treasure.

LISTEN TO GOOD MUSIC

Another emotional stabilizer is to listen to good music. "Music can soothe the savage beast," the saying goes, and when holiday panic sets in, the beast inside each of us shows its face. I keep several favorite Christmas tapes in the car and pop them into the tape deck when I go out to battle the traffic. The beautiful strains lift my spirits so that I am more patient in traffic jams and more generous in the face of other drivers' rudeness.

REACH OUT TO OTHERS

Perhaps the best thing we can do to strengthen ourselves emotionally is to reach out to others during this season.

One year, we called our local hospice and arranged to bring cards to the patients there. Mark and Laura created homemade

Christmas cards. My favorite greeting was seven-year-old Laura's message: "Jesus is always with you, so don't panic." As we brought these cards around to the patients, many were moved to tears. A visit from young children brings great joy to the elderly and the infirm. For Mark and Laura this experience was unforgettable—they knew that these folks were dying. Our visit took only several hours, yet it was the high point of my Christmas season.

Another year we bought Christmas presents for a needy family in the inner city. One cold day in mid-December, I drove downtown with the kids to deliver the gifts to the family. It was quite an eye-opening experience for all of us. The dingy stairwell reeked of urine, and the door opened to reveal a tiny apartment barren of furniture or toys. Several of the eight children were the ages of Mark and Laura. Their eyes grew as round as saucers as we pulled the gifts out of the bags and placed them under the small tree. As we prepared to go, the young single mother wrapped her arms around me in a speechless thank-you.

Experiences such as these put everything into perspective. Greed and self-centeredness come so naturally to all of us. Making these small sacrifices of time and energy to help the needy really helps us most of all. We get our focus off ourselves. Our own problems suddenly seem smaller. And the lessons our children learn are invaluable.

Spiritual

The most significant realm of our lives is the spiritual, which permeates everything we are. We cannot afford to neglect the spiritual, if we want to have a happy and meaningful Christmas.

SEEK AN ETERNAL PERSPECTIVE

First, we need to seek an eternal perspective. It helps to ask yourself, "What is really important?" According to the Bible, there are only two things on earth that are eternal: God's Word and people's souls. Remembering this truth helps me to keep my priorities in line.

DRAW NEAR TO GOD

Second, we need to draw near to God during this holy season. Four Sundays before Christmas begins the season of Advent, or "coming." Advent is a time of reflection and repentance. It helps us to prepare our hearts for the celebration of Christ's birth.

For my family, Advent has become a wonderful time of growth. Each evening we gather around the lighted Advent candles, read and discuss verses which point to Christ's coming, and sing a beloved Christmas carol. These moments of quiet worship and reflection instill in us a sense of peace that we carry with us throughout the month. More than that, as we meet Christ together each day, Jesus becomes the focus of our Christmas.

Take time out each day to meet Christ one-on-one, as well. It helps me to remember that this is the most important thing I do each day. Only in Christ do I find the strength to meet the tasks and challenges of the day. Jesus Christ gives me purpose, perspective, and peace. When I find that I have become short-tempered with my family, ungrateful in my attitudes, or preoccupied with the unimportant, it is usually because I have been neglecting my relationship with the Lord. If I am growing in that all-important relationship, my other relationships seem to fall into place.

Perhaps this idea of a "relationship with Christ" is new to you. Take an honest look deep within you. Is there something missing? There is an emptiness within each of us that can be filled only with God himself. He made us to know him, and until we know him, we are incomplete. Advent is a perfect time to begin to get to know Jesus Christ.

You will seek me and find me when you seek me with all your heart. (Jer. 29:13)

Part 2

Advent Devotions

A Note to Parents

Our children were ages three and one when I began searching for a creative way to make our Christmas season Christ-centered, a way that involved and taught the children. Enter Skip Sellers, mother of six, grandmother of three. Although twenty years my senior, Skip and I were kindred spirits. The blessing for me was that Skip had already experienced the stage of life into which I was now entering. It was Skip's Advent tree that inspired me to develop my own family Advent tree and devotions.

The purpose of the Advent banner or Jesse tree is to provide a festive visual aid for young children which will teach at the same time as it adds to the fun of brief family devotions. It is based on the traditional Advent calendars which many of us had as children. Each day of December, a circle is added to the tree. On each circle is a symbol that ties in with the Scripture passage for the day.

The Advent banner goes with chapter 4, Advent Devotions Year 1 (pp. 27–75). The Jesse tree goes with chapter 5, Advent Devotions Year 2 (pp. 77–129). Instructions for making these are given on pages 143–50. Patterns for the symbols are also included on pages 155–74.

If your children are older, or you simply do not have time to make the Advent banner or any of the simpler options suggested, don't worry. The family devotions for Advent work just fine on their own.

Do not feel that your family must do every part of each devotional. In the case of families with small children, this would be a mistake. Pint-sized people have pint-sized attention spans. Devotions work only if they are brief and keep children involved. That is why a visual aid (like the Advent banner) is helpful.

Also, I would recommend making or buying an Advent wreath. Children are fascinated by candles, and the flickering light contributes to the sense of the holiness of the time. Just be sure to take every safety precaution. (Instructions for making an Advent wreath are on pages 151–54.)

Involve small children by letting them put the symbols on the tree or by letting them blow out the Advent candles. Involve older children by letting them lead the devotional, read the Scripture, etc.

Each devotional includes these elements:

Explain—A real-life story introduces the theme or the passage.

Read—The central theme or question for each devotional is emphasized in a passage from the New International Version of the Bible.

Discuss—There are several questions for younger children and there are several for older children and adults. These are meant to encourage understanding and discussion.

Final Thought—This is a brief summary of truths or insights drawn from the passage.

Pray—These prayers are short and to the point. Don't feel limited to the suggested prayer. Encourage your children to pray extemporaneously as well.

Sing—Words to one or two verses of a Christmas or Advent hymn are printed out. The entire hymn, words and music, may be found in the Hymn section at the end of the book, pages 175–90.

Do—This section instructs you as to which symbol to find and place on your Advent banner.

Further Study for Adults—These are questions or suggestions for teens or adults who want to focus on these passages for their own personal quiet time or devotional time during Advent. Buy a blank book or use a spiral notebook or steno pad and call it your Advent journal. And get ready to grow!

Remember, do only those things that work with the ages and attention spans of your children. Feel free to change and adapt these ideas to suit the needs of your family. And don't forget to laugh and have fun!

Advent Devotions Year One

The Scripture readings in these devotions follow the general pattern of the Festival of Lessons and Carols that has been celebrated in King's College Chapel, Cambridge, England, since 1921. The passages selected summarize our relationship with God and recount the story of Christ's birth.

The devotionals follow this outline:

❄ December 1-3
Jesus—Eternal with the Father

❄ December 4-8
Jesus—Sent to Save Sinners

❄ December 9-17
Jesus—Spoken of by the Prophets

❄ December 18-24
Jesus—Born of the Virgin Mary

December 1
Jesus—Eternal with the Father

In the churchyards of many old churches are gravestones marking the graves of men, women, and children who lived long ago. On each of these stones we find words and dates. Can you guess what they might say? Below the name of the person, each marker records the date that the person was born and the date that he or she died. Each of our lives had a beginning. Do you know the date that you were born? Each of our lives will also have an earthly end—the day that we die.

What about Jesus? Did his life have a beginning? Did it start as a baby in Bethlehem? Let's find out by looking at something that Jesus told his best friend.

When Jesus lived on this earth, one of his best friends was named John. After Jesus went to heaven, John told people about Jesus. Years later, when John was very old, Jesus appeared to John and told him to write down everything Jesus told him. This is what John wrote.

Read—*Revelation 22:13*

I am the Alpha and the Omega, the First and the Last, the Beginning and the End.

Discuss

1. Alpha and Omega are the first and last letters of the Greek alphabet, like our A and Z. What did Jesus mean when he said that he is the A and the Z?
2. We began our lives when we started growing within our mothers. Was that true of Jesus? When did he begin?
3. Why is it important that Jesus is the First and the Last, the Beginning and the End?
4. Most people think of Christmas as the celebration of the birth of a baby, if they think of it at all. What difference does it make that this baby is the Alpha and the Omega?

Final Thought

We live our lives in time, marked by minutes, days, weeks, and years. Jesus said, "Before Abraham was, I AM." He exists in eternity, outside of time. How can we possibly understand this? Yet Jesus entered our world and let himself be chained to our time. In the face of such a mystery, the only adequate response is worship.

Pray

Lord Jesus, you always were and you always will be. We cannot understand it, but we believe it and give you thanks and praise. In your name, Amen.

Sing—*Oh, Come, All Ye Faithful* (p. 184)

> Oh, come, all ye faithful, Joyful and triumphant!
> Oh, come ye, oh, come ye to Bethlehem;
> Come and behold him, Born the king of angels:
> Oh, come, let us adore him,
> Christ, the Lord!

Do

Find the symbol of the Alpha and Omega. Place this on your Advent tree.

Further Study for Adults

Read John 8:48–59. Why did the Jewish leaders react so violently to Jesus's words? What was Jesus implying? What are the implications of this truth to your life?

December 2
Jesus—Eternal with the Father

Who is your best friend? Why is this person special? My very best friend (besides Jesus) is my husband, Jim. Even though he sees me at my very worst, he still loves me. We enjoy doing things together and we can tell each other anything. These are reasons we all like to have good friends. What do you suppose it was like to be one of Jesus's best friends when he lived on earth? No one has ever been such a good friend as Jesus is to all who will accept him.

Today's verses were written by Jesus's friend John. John lived with Jesus for three years and watched everything Jesus did. Perhaps he knew Jesus better than anyone else. This is what he said about Jesus.

Read—*John 1:1, 2, 14*

> In the beginning was the Word, and the Word was with God, and the Word was God. He was with God in the beginning . . . The Word became flesh and made his dwelling among us. We have seen his glory, the glory of the One and Only, who came from the Father, full of grace and truth.

Discuss

1. Who is the Word?
2. What does John say that he and the rest of the disciples saw?
3. What else do these verses tell us about him?
4. Discuss what it means that "The Word became flesh and made his dwelling among us."

Final Thought

In Mark 9:2–8 we read about a special time on a mountaintop when Jesus was changed before the eyes of Peter, James, and John. They saw him in his glory, his clothes dazzling white.

They heard God's words saying, "This is my Son, whom I love. Listen to him." They were given a small glimpse of the glory that Jesus left in order to come to earth to show us God's love and to die for us.

Pray

Dear Lord Jesus, thank you that you are God, yet you come to earth to show us what God is like. We would never have known, if you had not been born in Bethlehem that night. Thank you, Lord. In Jesus's precious name we pray, Amen.

Sing—*Oh, Come, All Ye Faithful* (p. 184)

> Yea, Lord, we greet thee,
> Born this happy morning,
> Jesus, to thee be glory given;
> Word of the Father,
> Now in flesh appearing:
> O come let us adore him,
> Christ, the Lord.

Do

Find the symbol of the Bible (the Word). Place this on your Advent tree.

Further Study for Adults

John, the beloved disciple, is the author of this verse. He also is the John who was with Jesus, Peter, and James on the Mount of Transfiguration. Read Mark 9:2–9. What did John observe? How might this have contributed to the picture he paints in the first chapter of his Gospel? Do a word study on "glory" throughout the upcoming weeks.

December 3
Jesus—Eternal with the Father

When my daughter Laura was in third grade, she made a topographic map of the state of Virginia. First we went out to a craft store and bought supplies. Carefully, she drew the outline of the state on a big board. Looking at a map which showed where the mountains were she began to scoop a paste made of flour and water onto the board, shaping the ridges and valleys. After waiting several days for the paste to dry, she got out her paints. Green went on the whole state, then blue for the rivers, ocean, and lakes. Finally, she placed white dots at the locations of all the major cities and labeled them in white.

What a feeling of accomplishment! Yet even with all her hard work, Laura did not create the state of Virginia. She had simply copied a map.

Think about Laura's project as you read these verses in Colossians about a project that Jesus had long before he came as a baby in Bethlehem. These verses describe Jesus.

Read—*Colossians 1:15, 16*

He is the image of the invisible God, the firstborn over all creation. For by him all things were created: things in heaven and on earth, visible and invisible, whether thrones or powers or rulers or authorities; all things were created by him and for him.

Discuss

1. What is it that Jesus did?
2. What things did Jesus create?
3. What does it mean that all things were created "by him and for him"?
4. What difference does it make to your view of Christ? The world? Your own life?

Final Thought

Jesus himself formed the hillsides on which the shepherds were watching the night of his birth. He hurled the stars into space, he created the angels who announced his birth, and he breathed life into man and woman at creation. When Jesus was born, the creator took the form of a creature—a tiny helpless baby. No wonder the heavens were full of his praise! What a mystery!

Pray

Lord, you created all things. You are so great. I know that I can trust you because you are the creator and ruler of the universe. In Jesus's name, Amen.

Sing—*Angels from the Realms of Glory* (p. 190)

> Angels, from the realms of glory,
> Wing your flight o'er all the earth;
> Once you sang creation's story,
> Now proclaim Messiah's birth:
> Come and worship, come and worship,
> Worship Christ, the newborn King.

Do

Find the symbol of the planets (creation). Place this on the Advent tree.

Further Study for Adults

Reread the story of creation (Genesis 1, 2), replacing the name "God" with "Jesus," based on Colossians 1:15–16. Write a prayer or song of praise to Jesus, the creator.

December 4
Jesus—Sent to Save Sinners

Many good books and stories begin with a problem. If so, the rest of the book probably tells how that problem is solved. When you read the book a second time, you already know how the problem is solved and you notice the clues that were given all along the way. The Bible does have this in common with other popular books: you don't have to read far to run into the problem.

Read—*Genesis 3:1–6, 14–15*

"Did God really say, 'You must not eat from any tree in the garden?'"

The woman said to the serpent, "We may eat fruit from the trees in the garden, but God did say, 'You must not eat fruit from the tree that is in the middle of the garden, and you must not touch it, or you will die.'"

"You will not surely die," the serpent said to the woman. "For God knows that when you eat of it your eyes will be opened, and you will be like God, knowing good and evil."

When the woman saw that the fruit of the tree was good for food and pleasing to the eye, and also desirable for gaining wisdom, she took some and ate it. She also gave some to her husband, who was with her, and he ate it.

. . . So the Lord God said to the serpent . . . "I will put enmity between you and the woman, and between your offspring and hers; he will crush your head and you will strike his heel."

Discuss

1. What was the problem that came up in these verses?
2. Whom do you think was to blame for this?
3. Read the rest of the chapter and discuss how each guilty party was punished.
4. Verse 15 contains the clue to the solution of this problem. Whom would God send to "crush the head" of Satan?

Final Thought

Think about it—the man and the woman had the perfect parent, God himself. They had the perfect environment, wonderful relationships, and meaningful work—yet they made the choice to disobey God. Would we have done any better?

Pray

Dear Lord God, forgive us for disobeying you. Thank you that even from the very beginning, your plan was to send Jesus as the solution to the problem of sin. In his name, Amen.

Sing—*Joy to the World* (p. 178)

> No more let sins and sorrow grow
> Nor thorns infest the ground;
> He comes to make his blessings flow
> Far as the curse is found.

Do

Find the symbol of the black heart. This stands for the sin, or wrong, in our lives. It is because of this sin that Jesus had to come to earth. Place this on the Advent tree.

Further Study for Adults

Read Romans 5:12–21. Divide your page into two columns. In the first column, list all that is said about Adam and the results of his choice. In the second column, list all that is said about Jesus Christ and the results of his coming into the world. Link the problems with the corresponding solutions.

December 5
Jesus—Sent to Save Sinners

When I was about six years old, I had an experience that I will never forget. My family was visiting our friends the Bengstons. After dinner my dad and I went for a walk around the block. As we approached the Bengstons' house, I asked Dad if I could walk around the block by myself. My dad immediately agreed. Off I went down the sidewalk feeling quite grown-up.

By the time I rounded the second corner, I was beginning to feel a bit confused. All the houses looked the same. Had we crossed a street before? I felt that we had. Carefully looking both ways, I crossed the street and walked slowly down the sidewalk, examining each house.

At last I spied a house that I was sure was the Bengstons'. I mounted the steps and knocked at the door. To my dismay, the woman who answered the door was not Mrs. Bengston. It wasn't the Bengstons' house at all! I asked her if she knew the Bengstons, but she didn't! The woman asked me to come inside, and assured me that she would find the Bengstons.

Her husband spoke to me while she made a phone call. They offered me orange soda but I politely refused. After all, I knew never to accept food from a stranger. In a little while, there was a knock at the door. A policeman stood in the doorway and behind him were the anxious faces of my mom and dad. With tears of relief, my parents took me in their arms.

Have you ever had a similar experience? Think about your experience as you read this verse from Isaiah.

Read—*Isaiah 53:6*

> We all, like sheep, have gone astray,
>> each of us has turned to his own way;
> and the Lord has laid on him
>> the iniquity of us all.

Discuss

1. The first part of this verse is a good definition of sin. How are we like a straying sheep?
2. What happened when I strayed and crossed the street? What happens to us when we stray from God's way?
3. What did God do about our sin?
4. What do you think this verse has to do with Christmas?

Final Thought

When I was lost, my parents were much more frightened than I was, simply because they knew the dangers of the world. Those who don't know Christ are usually blissfully ignorant of their danger. Thanks be to Jesus, the Good Shepherd, who rescued us.

Pray

Heavenly Father, thank you so much for sending your Son to take our sin on himself. Keep us on your path. In Jesus's name, Amen.

Sing—*Good Christian Friends, Rejoice* (p. 183)

Good Christian friends, rejoice,
With heart, and soul, and voice;
Now ye need not fear the grave:
Jesus Christ was born to save!
Calls you one and calls you all
To gain his everlasting hall.
Christ was born to save!

Do

Place the symbol of the cross on the Advent tree.

Further Study for Adults

Is there an area in your life in which you have been going your own way instead of God's way? Reflect on your relationships, your work situations, your use of time, your recreation.

December 6
Jesus—Sent to Save Sinners

A few years ago we had a puppy named Josie. She had white curly hair, rather scruffy-looking, and we loved her very much. We often called her "our little lamb," for she looked a bit like a lamb and was just as sweet. One afternoon, we forgot her in the backyard. Behind our house is a hilly road on which cars drive very fast. We spotted Josie across that busy street, sniffing around in a vacant lot. Quietly we crept to the edge of the street, but before we could cross to grab her, Josie looked up and saw us. Heedless of our cries to "Stay!" she bounded across the street. At that very moment, a car flew over the crest of the hill and hit her.

We rushed her to the vet, but he could not save her. We were heartbroken. We had made the dreadful mistake of forgetting her and she had paid the price with her life.

Recently, we have been learning about the problem of sin and the solution that God provided in Jesus Christ. Before Jesus came, God made a way for people's sins to be forgiven. Every year they had to kill (sacrifice) a perfect lamb on an altar. Now this lamb couldn't really take away their sins, but it did show how God would someday send a perfect sacrifice who would take away their sins forever. Killing the lamb was a way to show God that they believed his promise.

The verse that we read today tells us what John the Baptist said when he saw Jesus walking toward him.

Read—*John 1:29*

> The next day John saw Jesus coming toward him and said, "Look, the Lamb of God, who takes away the sin of the world!"

Discuss

  1. Have you ever done something that you wished you could undo?

2. What did John call Jesus?
3. Why did John call Jesus the Lamb of God?
4. Why did Jesus leave heaven and come into the world?

Final Thought

It was by Jesus's death and resurrection that our sins were taken away forever. Jesus lives, but our sins are dead! We still have to live with the consequences of our sins. No matter how sorry we were, we cannot bring back loved ones who are dead. We cannot undo things we have done. But Jesus brings healing and forgiveness to our hearts.

Pray

Thank you so much, Lord Jesus, for coming into the world to take away my sin. In your name, Amen.

Sing—*Once Again My Heart Rejoices* (p. 185)

> Hark! A voice from yonder manger,
> Soft and sweet, doth entreat,
> "Flee from woe and danger;
> Come and see; from all that grieves you
> You are freed; all you need
> I will surely give you."

Do

Find the symbol of the lamb. This reminds us that Jesus is the Lamb of God, who came to take away the sin of the world. Place this symbol on your Advent tree.

Further Study for Adults

If your life were videotaped, what would you be ashamed for others—particularly Jesus—to see? These are the sins that Jesus came to take away. Read Psalm 103. It is because of Jesus Christ's death that these verses apply to us. Reflect on the benefits that are ours because of the "Lamb of God, who takes away the sin of the world."

December 7
Jesus—Sent to Save Sinners

When you were a baby, your parents did lots of things to take care of you. They had to get up in the middle of the night and feed you. They had to watch over you every minute. When you were sick, they had to hold you and comfort you and sometimes stay up all night with you. It wasn't easy. Why do you think they did these things for you?

When I was a little girl, my mom always got up with me in the night when I was sick. She put cold washcloths on my forehead to bring down my fever. She lay down next to me in bed so that she was right there when I needed her. She supported my head as I hung it over the toilet when I had to throw up. Do you think that was fun for her? Not likely. Why did she do it then? The answer is simple—she loved me.

Love means being willing to sacrifice, give something up. We parents give up lots of things: sleep, comfort, exciting vacations, and peaceful evenings because we love our children.

Our heavenly Father loves us, even more than our earthly parents do. This verse tells us how he shows us his love.

Read—*1 John 4:9*

This is how God showed his love among us: He sent his one and only Son into the world that we might live through him.

Discuss

1. How did God show us his love?
2. Do you think this was a hard thing to do? Why?
3. What would be the hardest sacrifice for you to make?
4. Why did God make this supreme sacrifice? How should we respond?

Final Thought

In a few years, our sons will be leaving home for college. That will be a new kind of sacrifice for us. How difficult it will be, yet it pales in comparison to the separation that the Father felt during the ultimate separation which came when Jesus bore our sins on the cross. How great is the love of God for us that he would make such a sacrifice!

Pray

Heavenly Father, thank you for your great love for us. You loved us so much that you did the hardest thing you could do—you gave up your one and only Son. In his name we pray, Amen.

Sing—*O Little Town of Bethlehem* (p. 179)

How silently, how silently,
The wondrous Gift is given!
So God imparts to human hearts
The blessings of his heaven.
No ear may hear his coming,
But in this world of sin,
Where meek souls will receive him, still
The dear Christ enters in.

Do

Find the symbol of the heart. Color it red, for this reminds us of God's love for us—love that cost him his one and only Son. Place this symbol on the Advent tree.

Further Study for Adults

What sacrifices do you make for those you love? What sacrifices do your loved ones make for you? How can you respond to God's sacrifice in Jesus Christ? What are some selfish indulgences that you should sacrifice because of your love for him?

December 8
Jesus—Sent to Save Sinners

Christmas is a time of fun secrets, isn't it? Sometimes it is hard to keep secrets. When our daughter Laura was little, we had to keep all the gifts hidden from her, otherwise, somehow, the secret would pop out. She got so excited about everyone else's gifts and the fact that she knew something that someone else didn't that she couldn't resist giving hints. As you probably know, a hint from a youngster is usually enough to let the cat out of the bag!

Secrets and gifts seem to go together. In our verse for today, there is a secret and a gift. I will tell you about the secret, but you will have to figure out the gift.

One night, a man named Nicodemus came secretly to ask Jesus some questions. This meeting was a secret, not for happy reasons, but because Nicodemus was afraid. He didn't want anyone to see him talking to Jesus, because he knew that he would get into trouble. The men he worked with hated Jesus. The good thing about Nicodemus is that he didn't just hate Jesus along with his friends. He wanted to find out more about him.

Read—*John 3:16*

> For God so loved the world that he gave his one and only Son,
> that whoever believes in him shall not perish but have eternal life.

Discuss

1. Can you figure out what the gift is in this verse? Who gave it?
2. God loves us so much that he gave us his most precious gift. What do you do with the gifts under the Christmas tree? What do you think God wants us to do with his gift?
3. Why did the Father send Jesus into the world?
4. What do you think it means to "believe in Him"?

Final Thought

The story of Nicodemus has a happy ending. When the other Jewish leaders wanted to arrest Jesus, Nicodemus spoke up so that Jesus would be treated fairly (see John 7:50–52). Then after Jesus died on the cross, it was Nicodemus who, along with Joseph of Arimathea, took Jesus's body, anointed it with myrrh and aloes, wrapped it in linen, and buried it in Joseph's tomb (see John 19:38–42). By this time, Nicodemus no longer worried about what the Jewish leaders thought. He just wanted to show his love for Jesus. It seems that he had finally accepted Jesus's gift of eternal life.

Pray

Dearest Father, thank you for giving us your Son Jesus so that we can live forever with you. Right now I take this gift and ask Jesus to be my Lord and Savior. In Jesus's name, Amen.

Sing—O *Little Town of Bethlehem* (p. 179)

O holy Child of Bethlehem,
Descend to us, we pray;
Cast out our sin, and enter in,
Be born in us today.
We hear the Christmas angels
The great glad tidings tell;
O come to us, abide with us,
Our lord Emmanuel! Amen.

Do

Find the symbol of the gift. Place it on your Advent tree.

Further Study for Adults

Write a list of all the blessings that God has given you as a part of his gift of eternal life in Jesus. Pray for a grateful heart during this Advent season.

December 9
Jesus—Spoken of by the Prophets

Let's play blindman's bluff. Get a kerchief and tie it around one family member's eyes so she cannot see. Twirl her around until she doesn't remember which direction is which. Now pick another family member to give her directions. He needs to make sure that she does not bump into anything. Guide her by voice around the room or around the main floor of your home.

Now let's talk about it. What was it like to be blind? What was difficult about it? Were you afraid of anything?

It may be fun for a short game, but it would not be fun to be blind permanently. Imagine never again seeing a sunset. Easy tasks would be difficult and full of frustration. Even worse, you would never again see the faces of your loved ones.

The Bible often talks about darkness and light. You may remember that Jesus said, "I am the light of the world." Many years before Jesus was born, when God wanted to give his people a message of hope and light in their dark times, he spoke to his special helpers. These helpers were called prophets. A prophet would write down God's message, then tell it to the people. One of God's prophets was Isaiah, who lived seven hundred years before Jesus. God told Isaiah many things about the Savior that he was going to send.

Read—*Isaiah 9:2*

> The people walking in darkness
> have seen a great light;
> on those living in the land of the shadow of death
> a light has dawned.

Discuss

1. What is it like to walk in complete darkness?
2. What does light do to the darkness?

3. How is sin like darkness?
4. Why is Jesus called the light?

Final Thought

We have a glimpse of heaven in the book of Revelation. We read in Revelation 22:5, "There will be no more night. They will not need the light of a lamp or the light of the sun, for the Lord God will give them light." It is only because Jesus came to earth and died for us that we will be able to see heaven.

Pray

Thank you, Lord, that you are perfectly good—there is no sin in you. You are like the light that chases away the darkness of evil. Fill us with your light and your goodness, Lord. In Jesus's name, Amen.

Sing—*Hark! The Herald Angels Sing* (p. 180)

Hail, the heaven-born Prince of Peace!
Hail, the sun of Righteousness!
Light and life to all he brings,
Risen with healing in his wings.
Mild he lays his glory by,
Born that we no more may die,
Born to raise each child of earth,
Born to give us second birth.
Hark! The herald angels sing,
"Glory to the newborn King!"

Do

Find the symbol of the candle. Place it on your Advent tree.

Further Study for Adults

Begin a word study of light. Every time you come across the word "light" in the Bible, especially during Advent, write out the verse in this section of your Advent journal. Then write how it is used and its significance in that context.

December 10
Jesus—Spoken of by the Prophets

When I was in college, I spent one summer at a Christian camp in the Rocky Mountains. As a part of the program, each group of campers and their counselors went on an overnight backpacking trip. After a long day of hiking, we finally reached a flat area near a rushing stream overshadowed by tall pine trees. We set up our "tents," which looked to me like black plastic garbage bags with the bottoms cut open. Each of us had one of these "tube tents," made by stringing a rope through them and tying the rope ends to two trees, then anchoring the sides with rocks.

After supper and conversation around the campfire, rain started to fall. We all dashed for our tube tents and huddled inside. It was pitch dark, and the raindrops sounded like hailstones on my plastic tent. I was just starting to drift off to sleep when a loud sound jarred me awake. A voice over a megaphone was shouting through the thunder and rain. Who could it be? We were miles from civilization. No one in our group had a megaphone. I couldn't understand the words, but the shouting continued. I was terrified.

Several people from the group tried to investigate without success. Finally I fell asleep. Morning dawned bright and fair, and over breakfast we discussed the adventure of the previous night, trying to solve the mystery. Later that day, we learned that a work crew from camp had felt sorry for us out in the rain and had come to encourage us by reading Bible verses over a megaphone!

It is frightening to be in the dark, especially when you hear sounds that you don't understand.

Read—*Isaiah 60:1, 2*

> Arise, shine, for your light has come,
> and the glory of the Lord rises upon you.
> See, darkness covers the earth
> and thick darkness is over the peoples,
> but the Lord rises upon you
> and his glory appears over you.

Discuss

1. Where was the darkness?
2. Who is the light?
3. What words are repeated in these verses?
4. Can you find any opposites? What do they represent?

Final Thought

In the Bible, darkness often means sin and hopelessness. Glory refers to God's presence. When Jesus was born, God's presence came to earth in a special way. Jesus brings life, hope, and freedom.

Pray

Thank you, Lord Jesus, that you came to bring light to a dark world. Help me to be a light to all the people that I know, by telling them about your love. In Jesus's name, Amen.

Sing—*Joy to the World* (p. 178)

He rules the world with truth and grace,
And makes the nations prove
The glories of his righteousness,
And wonders of his love.

Do

Find the symbol of the sun. Place this symbol on your Advent tree.

Further Study for Adults

Read Isaiah 60:1–3, 17–22, looking for the theme of light. Add these verses to your word study on light. These verses, although addressed to Zion, find their fulfillment in the new people of God, those who have been redeemed by Christ. Which of these promises have been fulfilled already in your life? How? Which ones do you look forward to seeing fulfilled?

December 11
Jesus—Spoken of by the Prophets

A family that truly loves the Lord can make a difference in the lives of many people. One such family in my life was the family of Gordy and Bonnie Addington. The Addingtons were missionaries in Hong Kong for many years. At that time the Addingtons had ten children, ranging in age from college to kindergarten. I had never seen a family who got up every morning at 6:00 to have devotions together around the breakfast table! Tim taught me how to study the Bible and how to help others grow in their relationship with Christ.

The Addingtons had a tremendous influence on me at a crucial time in my life. They helped me see how important the Christian family is in showing God's love to a world of lonely people.

In the Bible, we read about Abraham and the promises God made to him concerning his family, who would be God's special people. Abraham's family grew into a nation, the nation of Israel, or the Jews. Everyone else was called a Gentile. God promised Abraham wonderful things for his family, the Jews. But he also promised Abraham that his family would bring happiness to the whole world, including the Gentiles. This verse tells how.

Read—*Isaiah 49:6*

> It is too small a thing for you to be my servant
> to restore the tribes of Jacob
> and bring back those of Israel I have kept.
> I will also make you a light for the Gentiles,
> that you may bring my salvation to the ends of the
> earth.

Discuss

1. God is talking to those Jews who would believe in Jesus. What did God promise that they would do?

2. Where would this special family bring God's salvation?
3. What is the salvation that God is referring to in this verse?
4. Whom can you tell about Jesus this week?

Final Thought

One important way that we shine for Jesus is to have a loving family. When others see a family that loves each other and treats each other with respect, they are amazed. In this day and age, that is exceptional! On the other hand, if Christian families are no different than any other family, we don't have much to offer, do we? Let us commit ourselves to treating our family members with kindness and respect, so that those around us can see that Jesus makes the difference in our lives.

Pray

Dear Lord, you came to save us and we are so thankful. Help us to show our thankfulness by loving our family as well as our friends and neighbors. Let them see the difference that you make in our lives. In Jesus's name, Amen.

Sing—*Silent Night* (p. 181)

> Silent night, holy night! Son of God, love's pure Light
> Radiant beams from your holy face,
> With the dawn of redeeming grace,
> Jesus, Lord at your birth, Jesus, Lord, at your birth.

Do

Place the symbol of the trumpet on your Advent tree.

Further Study for Adults

Reflect on the families that God has used in your life to draw you closer to him, whether it be your own family, or others, or both. Write a thank-you note to God for these families.

December 12
Jesus—Spoken of by the Prophets

One January evening in 1981, an Air Florida jet carrying hundreds of people took off from Washington National Airport and began its ascent over the icy Potomac River. Suddenly the plane began to fall. It crashed into a bridge packed with rush hour commuters, sending cars plummeting into the river. The plane plunged nose first into the water. Passengers on board fought their way out of the plane as it filled with freezing water.

A young man standing on the banks of the river apparently saw the crash and wasted no time in diving in to save the lives of drowning passengers. A number of people were saved by the courageous efforts of this man. Who was this young man? No one knows to this day. Did he drown while saving others? Did he slip away unnoticed after his heroic work? Was he an angel? Whoever he was, he saved several from an icy, terrifying death.

We all hope that we never face death in such a terrifying manner, yet we will all die. And we all need a Savior. Hundreds of years before Jesus was born, God promised his people a Savior.

Read—*Isaiah 9:6*

> For to us a child is born,
> to us a son is given,
> and the government will be on his shoulders.
> And he will be called
> Wonderful Counselor, Mighty God,
> Everlasting Father, Prince of Peace.

Discuss

1. What are some of the names that you have been called? Do you think it is important what people call you?
2. What names would this child-Savior be called?
3. Tell what each of these names means.

4. What do we learn about the Savior from this verse?

Final Thought

In the Bible, names tell about who a person is or what he will do. These names show who Jesus was and what he came to earth to do. Isn't it wonderful that our Savior does not want to remain a mystery to us? He wants us to know him! The better we know him, the more we can trust him with our lives.

Pray

We praise you, Lord Jesus, that you are the Wonderful Counselor, the Mighty God, the Everlasting Father, and the Prince of Peace. Help me to remember this, and to trust you with my life. In Jesus's name, Amen.

Sing—*Joy to the World* (p. 178)

> Joy to the world, the Lord is come;
> Let earth receive its King;
> Let every heart prepare him room,
> And heaven and nature sing.

Do

Find the symbol of the dove. This reminds us that Jesus is the Prince of Peace. Place this symbol on your Advent tree.

Further Study for Adults

Reflect on each of these names. Notice the attributes of God in each name as it applies to Christ. Put these names in your own words, perhaps looking up terms in a dictionary or Bible dictionary. Do you really believe that Jesus is all these things? How is this belief showing itself in your life?

December 13
Jesus—Spoken of by the Prophets

In recent years, the British royalty has been much talked about in papers, magazines, and books, with rumors of scandals, affairs, and failed marriages. On the surface, the life of a prince or princess seems so glorious, living in a palace with servants at your beck and call, parties to attend, limousines for even the smallest errand, and beautiful clothes to wear. Yet, in the royal family of England we have seen glimpses of a deeply unhappy family with very little understanding of love. Are our leaders any better? Sometimes it seems impossible to find a leader who is truly a good person, who will keep his promises, and who is fair in all his dealings and just in his approach to governing. These verses tell how Jesus will someday rule the world.

Read—*Isaiah 9:7*

> Of the increase of his government and peace
> there will be no end.
> He will reign on David's throne
> and over his kingdom
> establishing and upholding it
> with justice and righteousness
> from that time on and forever.
> The zeal of the LORD Almighty
> will accomplish this.

Discuss

1. What kind of a king will Jesus be?
2. If we love and obey Jesus, then he is our king right now. What can you do today to love and obey Jesus?
3. How will Christ's rule be different than the current world governments?
4. What do you think it means that "the zeal of the Lord Almighty will accomplish this"?

Final Thought

We all long for leaders who tell the truth, who are good and wise, and who will accomplish things that will be fair and helpful to all people. Jesus is that kind of leader! Are we allowing him to rule our lives?

Pray

Dear Lord, I want you to be my king—every day of my life. Please help me to love and obey you as my king. In Jesus's name, Amen.

Sing—*Joy to the World* (p. 178)

> Joy to the world! The Savior reigns!
> Let all their songs employ,
> While fields and floods, rocks, hills, and plains
> Repeat the sounding joy.
>
> He rules the world with truth and grace,
> And makes the nations prove
> The glories of his righteousness,
> And wonders of his love.

Do

Find the symbol of the crown. This reminds us that Jesus will rule the world someday as king. If we trust and obey him, he is our king today. Place this symbol on your Advent tree.

Further Study for Adults

Read Psalm 85. What similarities do you find between this psalm and Isaiah 9:7? Look particularly at verses 8–13. In these verses, several of God's attributes are personified. What are they pictured doing? How do these expressions find their fulfillment in Christ?

December 14
Jesus—Spoken of by the Prophets

Have you ever gotten a puppy or a kitten? Several months after the terrible day upon which our puppy Josie had been run over and killed we found ourselves on the way to visit a dog breeder. She had a tiny female puppy for us. We were tense with excitement as the woman went to the kennel to get the puppy. It was love at first sight. The puppy was so small that she fit into cupped hands. She almost looked more like a guinea pig or baby rabbit! She had a square jaw, fuzzy, soft hair, and a cuddly yet playful manner. It didn't take us long to decide that she was the puppy for us.

The puppy was too young to leave her mother, so we had to wait six more weeks. By that time, she had grown quite a bit. We cradled her in our arms and carried her out to the car. Mark and Laura fought over who would hold her during the ride home. Mark won, but his reward was that as soon as we drove into our driveway, the puppy threw up on him!

We named the puppy Casey. During the next several months, she needed lots of love and attention. We watched over her every minute. She was smart and eager to please, so house-breaking was relatively easy, but it required time and attentiveness. We loved her and happily cared for her.

In biblical times, that same kind of loving relationship was seen between shepherds and their sheep. God used that image when He told Isaiah more about what the Savior would be like.

Read—*Isaiah 40:11*

> He tends his flock like a shepherd:
> He gathers the lambs in his arms
> and carries them close to his heart;
> he gently leads those that have young.

Discuss

1. Who is the shepherd? Who is the flock?
2. What do we learn about what the Savior would be like?
3. Was Jesus like this?
4. How does Jesus care for you like a shepherd?

Final Thought

As beautiful and tender as this picture is, it is only a faint glimpse of the great love that Jesus has for us.

Pray

Dear Jesus, you are so gentle and kind to us. Thank you for loving us and caring for us like a shepherd. In your name we pray, Amen.

Sing—*Once Again My Heart Rejoices* (p. 185)

> Hark! A voice from yonder manger,
> Soft and sweet, doth entreat,
> "Flee from woe and danger;
> Brethren, come; from all that grieves you
> You are freed; all you need
> I will surely give you."

Do

Find the symbol of the shepherd's staff. This reminds us that Jesus is the Good Shepherd. Place this symbol on the Advent tree.

Further Study for Adults

Read John 10:1–18. Several words and themes are repeated in these shepherd images. Let's look at these, keeping in mind the prophecy of Isaiah 40:11. "I am . . ." To what did Jesus liken himself? Why? "Voice." What did Jesus say about voices? Why did he make such a point of this? "Life." Look at each use of this word. How are they related?

December 15
Jesus—Spoken of by the Prophets

When we moved into our current home, we discovered that the two huge old holly bushes that grew beside our house were almost dead. We cut them down, planning to dig out the stumps and plant new shrubs the following year.

Spring arrived, and we were astonished to find new shoots growing out of the ground where the old bushes had been. Budding leaves unfolded into shiny, bright green ovals, healthy and young. We decided to wait and see what happened to these new shoots.

The new branches grew thicker, and branched further. Soon it became obvious that we had new plants growing from the old roots. It has now been six years since we cut down those dead holly bushes. The new bushes have grown steadily each year.

Read—*Isaiah 11:1–3*

> A shoot will come up from the stump of Jesse;
> from his roots a Branch will bear fruit.
> The Spirit of the LORD will rest on him—
> the Spirit of wisdom and of understanding,
> the Spirit of counsel and of power,
> the Spirit of knowledge and of the fear of the LORD—
> and he will delight in the fear of the LORD.

Discuss

1. Do you know who Jesse was? Read 1 Samuel 16:10–13.
2. Jesse's family is compared to a bush or tree which has been cut off at the stump. The reason it was cut off is that David's family did not continue to rule as the royal family of Israel. What promise does God make about the stump of Jesse?
3. What do these verses tell us about this Branch?

4. Jesus was the branch from the family of David. Matthew 1 and Luke 3:23–31 show that Jesus did come from David's family. What does this tell us about how God keeps his promises?

Final Thought

When Jesus was a little boy, his family went to live in the town of Nazareth. In Matthew 2:23, Matthew tells us that this was so that the prophecy could be fulfilled that said, "He will be called a Nazarene." Nazarene comes from the Hebrew word *neser*, which means "branch."

Pray

Heavenly Father, thank you for keeping all your promises. And thank you that Jesus knew everything and happily obeyed you. Help me to happily obey you today, Lord. In Jesus's name, Amen.

Sing—*Oh, Come, Oh, Come, Emmanuel* (p. 176)

O come, strong Branch of Jesse, free
Your own from Satan's tyranny;
From depths of hell your people save,
And give them vict'ry o'er the grave.
Rejoice! Rejoice! Emmanuel
Shall come to you, O Israel.

Do

Find the symbol of the stump and the branch. The stump is the family of Jesse and David. Jesus is the branch that grew out of this family, just as God promised. Place this symbol on the Advent tree.

Further Study for Adults

Read God's promise to David in 2 Samuel 7:1–17. How was verse 16 fulfilled? Now read David's response, verses 18–29. What can we learn here about God, David, prayer, ourselves?

December 16
Jesus—Spoken of by the Prophets

Where were you born? I was born in Minneapolis, Minnesota. On three occasions in recent years, I have traveled outside the United States. In each case, I have had to fill out a tourist information card telling my reason for visiting, my destination, and my place of birth. This information is crucial in establishing my identity. The courthouse in Minneapolis has a record of my birth along with the names of my parents. If someone wants to check, they can call the courthouse of the city in which I was born.

About seven hundred years before the birth of Christ, God told the prophet Micah where the Savior would be born.

Read—*Micah 5:2*

> But you, Bethlehem Ephrathah,
> though you are small among the
> clans of Judah,
> out of you will come for me
> one who will be ruler over Israel,
> whose origins are from of old,
> from ancient times.

Discuss

1. God is talking to the little village of Bethlehem. What message does he have for Bethlehem?
2. Where was Jesus born? Why was he born there—did Mary live there? God had it all planned out. Read Luke 2:1–4.
3. This verse comes into play in the Christmas story. Read Matthew 2:1–8, 16–18. Who remembered this verse from Micah? Who was helped by this verse? How did trouble come of it?
4. What does this tell us about God's plans and purposes?

Final Thought

We think of our lives in terms of past, present, and future. It isn't that way with God. He is outside of time. We need to remember this when we wonder about God's plans and purposes. We cannot understand this about God, because he is so different from us in this respect. But we can accept it and respond by worshiping such a great God and entrusting him with our lives.

Pray

Thank you, Lord, that you planned every little detail of how and where Jesus would be born. Nothing happened by accident. You are a great and wonderful God. We praise you in Jesus's name, Amen.

Sing—O *Little Town of Bethlehem* (p. 179)

O little town of Bethlehem,
How still we see thee lie!
Above thy deep and dreamless sleep
The silent stars go by;
Yet in thy dark streets shineth
The everlasting Light;
The hopes and fears of all the years
Are met in thee tonight.

Do

Find the symbol of the Bethlehem building. This reminds us that Jesus was born in Bethlehem, just as God had said many years before. Place this symbol on your Advent tree.

Further Study for Adults

Look again at the passage in Matthew 2. How was Herod's belief different from the Magi's belief? Now read Romans 8. What promises does God give us in this chapter? Do you believe that God will keep his promises? How does your belief translate into action?

December 17
Jesus—Spoken of by the Prophets

The summer after I turned sixteen, my mom and I drove across Canada with my two younger sisters. We entered Canada at Sault Ste. Marie and headed east for Quebec, where we planned to go south to Vermont. In those days, the highway across western Canada was just a two-lane road most of the way. It was impossible to get lost. We were either going east or west. There were no other roads.

Then we came to Quebec. Mom was driving and I had the map. The two-lane highway had become an eight-lane superhighway, full of cloverleafs. And in Quebec, all the signs were in French!

At that point in my life, I had not taken any French; nor had my sisters. Three years of junior high Spanish was not sufficient for reading French rapidly! Needless to say, we lost our way. Fortunately, we were able to find some helpful, English-speaking Canadians at a gas station who pointed us in the right direction.

We depend on signs tremendously. Next time you go anywhere in your car, count the number of signs you see. You will be amazed. Signs give us information and help us make choices.

God knew that when he sent his Son to earth, people would need to have some signs in order to recognize him. Here God gives Isaiah a sign about the birth of this Savior that would come seven hundred years later.

Read—*Isaiah 7:14*

> Therefore the Lord himself will give you a sign: The virgin will be with child and will give birth to a son, and will call him Immanuel.

Discuss

1. What was the sign that people should look for?
2. What would this special baby boy be called?

3. What does the name Immanuel mean? Read Matthew 1:23.

4. How does this name fit Jesus?

Final Thought

God had Jesus's birth planned down to the last detail. I have heard it suggested that every young Jewish girl wondered if she might be the young woman spoken of in this verse. Especially if she loved God and believed his promises. Can you imagine how Mary must have felt when she learned from the angel that she was the one? She would be the mother of Immanuel, "God with us"!

Pray

How wonderful you are, Lord! Thank you for coming to earth to be one of us! In Jesus's name, Amen.

Sing—*Oh, Come, All Ye Faithful* (p. 184)

Oh, come, all ye faithful, Joyful and triumphant!
Oh, come ye, oh, come ye to Bethlehem;
Come and behold him, Born the king of angels:
Oh, come, let us adore him,
Christ, the Lord!

Do

Find the symbol of the manger. This reminds us of the miracle of Jesus's birth, as the prophets foretold. Place this symbol on your Advent tree.

Further Study for Adults

Review all the prophecies concerning the Christ that we have referred to over the past nine days. It may be helpful to write out a list of prophecies and how Jesus fulfilled them. What does this teach us about the character of God? Write a prayer praising God for these attributes.

December 18
Jesus—Born of the Virgin Mary

As a high school senior, it didn't take long for me to realize that I did not belong in physics. The teacher, Mr. Detloff, was very disappointed when I told him of my decision to drop his class. At the close of each year, Mr. Detloff chose one graduating senior to receive a college scholarship. *Well, that's one scholarship I know I won't get,* I thought. Can you imagine my surprise when my name was called? I stumbled forward and shook Mr. Detloff's hand, taking the check he handed me. I don't know to this day why he chose me. For some reason, Mr. Detloff cared about my future.

Let's read about a young woman chosen by God for a special task.

Read—*Luke 1:26–38*

> In the sixth month, God sent the angel Gabriel to Nazareth, a town in Galilee, to a virgin pledged to be married to a man named Joseph, a descendant of David. The virgin's name was Mary. The angel went to her and said, "Greetings, you who are highly favored! The Lord is with you."
>
> Mary was greatly troubled at his words and wondered what kind of greeting this might be. But the angel said to her, "Do not be afraid, Mary, you have found favor with God. You will be with child and give birth to a son, and you are to give him the name Jesus. He will be great and will be called the Son of the Most High. The Lord God will give him the throne of his father David, and he will reign over the house of Jacob forever; his kingdom will never end."
>
> "How will this be," Mary asked the angel, "since I am a virgin?"
>
> The angel answered, "The Holy Spirit will come upon you, and the power of the Most High will overshadow you. So the holy one to be born will be called the Son of God. Even Elizabeth your relative is going to have a child in her old age, and she who was said to be barren is in her sixth month. For nothing is impossible with God."

"I am the Lord's servant," Mary answered. "May it be to me as you have said." Then the angel left her.

Discuss

1. What message did Gabriel bring to Mary?
2. How would you feel if you were Mary?
3. What did Mary say?
4. Was this a good answer? Why?

Final Thought

We, like Mary, have been chosen by God—not because of what we have done, but simply because he wants us to belong to him, to love and serve him.

Pray

Dear Lord, nothing is impossible for you. Make me obedient to you, like Mary was. Help me not to be afraid, but simply to trust and obey you. In Jesus's name, Amen.

Sing—*Silent Night* (p. 181)

Silent night, holy night,
All is calm, all is bright
Round yon virgin mother and child.
Holy Infant, so tender and mild,
Sleep in heavenly peace.

Do

Find the symbol of Mary, Jesus's mother. Place this symbol on your Advent tree.

Further Study for Adults

What promises was Mary given? How did the angel encourage her? What does Mary's response tell us about her?

December 19
Jesus—Born of the Virgin Mary

Sometimes when I am worried about something, I will dream about it. Does this ever happen to you? Perhaps I am preparing to speak before a large group of people. Sometimes I dream that I have missed my appointment or am late, and, upon arriving, find myself totally unprepared for what I am supposed to do. Everything seems to be going wrong! What a relief it is to wake up after a nightmare like that. I feel as though I have been given a second chance!

Today's passage is about a dream that Joseph had when he was worried about something. Joseph's dream was special, however. God actually sent his angel into Joseph's dream to deliver a message.

Read—*Matthew 1:18–24*

This is how the birth of Jesus Christ came about: His mother Mary was pledged to be married to Joseph, but before they came together, she was found to be with child through the Holy Spirit. Because Joseph her husband was a righteous man and did not want to expose her to public disgrace, he had in mind to divorce her quietly.

But after he had considered this, an angel of the Lord appeared to him in a dream and said, "Joseph son of David, do not be afraid to take Mary home as your wife, because what is conceived in her is from the Holy Spirit. She will give birth to a son, and you are to give him the name Jesus, because he will save his people from their sins."

All this took place to fulfill what the Lord had said through the prophet: "The virgin will be with child and will give birth to a son, and they will call him Immanuel"—which means, "God with us."

When Joseph woke up, he did what the angel of the Lord had commanded him and took Mary home as his wife.

Discuss

1. What reason did the angel give for naming the baby Jesus?
2. Jesus means "The Lord saves." Why does this name fit Jesus?
3. How did Joseph respond to this dream?
4. How can we be more like Joseph?

Final Thought

I have always admired Joseph. He seems to me to be a man of integrity. He wanted to do the right thing, and he also had a compassionate heart. As soon as he learned God's will, he wasted no time in doing it.

Pray

We are so thankful that you came to save us, Lord Jesus. Help us to show our thankfulness by obeying you like Joseph did. In your name, Amen.

Sing—*Good Christian Friends, Rejoice* (p. 183)

Good Christian friends, rejoice,
With heart, and soul, and voice;
Now we need not fear the grave:
Jesus Christ was born to save!
Calls you one and calls you all
To gain his everlasting hall.
Christ was born to save!

Do

Find the symbol of Joseph. Place it on your Advent tree.

Further Study for Adults

How do you suppose Joseph was feeling about this situation? What do we learn of his character by how he handled the situation? How do these traits make him a good choice for raising Jesus? How can you grow in these qualities?

December 20
Jesus—Born of the Virgin Mary

Do you ever watch the Charlie Brown Christmas special on television? I love to watch Linus, dressed in his striped bathrobe on the stage, playing one of the shepherds. Solemnly, he recites from memory the beloved verses from Luke 2—the story describing the birth of Jesus Christ, our Lord and Savior. Some of us have heard these verses every Christmas of our lives. If we are not careful, we can become so familiar with them that we forget to listen. This time, close your eyes and try to imagine what it was like.

Read—*Luke 2:1–7*

In those days Caesar Augustus issued a decree that a census should be taken of the entire Roman world. (This was the first census that took place while Quirinius was governor of Syria.) And everyone went to his own town to register.

So Joseph also went up from the town of Nazareth in Galilee to Judea, to Bethlehem the town of David, because he belonged to the house and line of David. He went there to register with Mary, who was pledged to be married to him and was expecting a child. While they were there, the time came for the baby to be born, and she gave birth to her firstborn, a son. She wrapped him in cloths and placed him in a manger, because there was no room for them in the inn.

Discuss

1. What was it like for Mary and Joseph that night?
2. Why do you think God chose to become poor and homeless instead of rich?
3. Why do you think Luke included all the details about Caesar and the census in his account?
4. Caesar had no regard for God, nor was he trying to fulfill prophecy when he issued this decree. He had his own

reasons. Yet God worked through Caesar to accomplish his own purposes. What does that tell us about how God works?

Final Thought

These verses are very simple and straightforward, just as Mary and Joseph were simple people. God is not impressed with the great and mighty Caesars of this world. He looks for simple Marys and Josephs who are listening for his voice and ready to do what he says.

Pray

Thank you, Lord, that you came as a poor, homeless child. Let my love for you be pure and simple, too, Lord Jesus. In your name, Amen.

Sing—*Away in a Manger* (p. 188)

Away in a manger, no crib for his bed,
The little Lord Jesus laid down his sweet head;
The stars in the sky looked down where he lay,
The little Lord Jesus, asleep on the hay.

Do

Find the symbol of the baby Jesus. Place this symbol on your Advent tree.

Further Study for Adults

Caesar Augustus was the greatest emperor of the most powerful and influential government this world has known. Yet his decree was merely God's tool. How does this truth affect your view of the world? Your life?

December 21
Jesus—Born of the Virgin Mary

Last summer our family went camping in the mountains of south-western Virginia. Our tent was pitched in a meadow on top of a mountain. In the evening, we watched as the sunlight faded and the stars appeared. Soon the sky was velvety black and the stars dazzling white. We were amazed at how many thousands of stars we could see. This must have been what it was like for the shepherds on the hillside that night. But their night didn't end with a view of the stars! The stars were just the warm-up act for the angels!

Read—*Luke 2:8–14*

And there were shepherds living out in the fields nearby, keeping watch over their flocks at night. An angel of the Lord appeared to them, and the glory of the Lord shone around them, and they were terrified. But the angel said to them, "Do not be afraid. I bring you good news of great joy that will be for all the people. Today in the town of David a Savior has been born to you; he is Christ the Lord. This will be a sign to you: you will find a baby wrapped in cloths and lying in a manger."

Suddenly a great company of the heavenly host appeared with the angel, praising God and saying,

"Glory to God in the highest
and on earth peace to men on whom his favor rests."

Discuss

1. Describe what the shepherds saw that night.
2. Shepherds were not very important people. Why do you think God sent his angels to these poor shepherds?
3. These flocks were most likely the sheep who would be sacrificed in the temple. What does this tell us about why God might have appeared to these shepherds?
4. What do you learn about the Savior from the message delivered by the angel?

Final Thought

Jesus came as the good shepherd, who would lay down his life for the sheep (see John 10:11). He also came as the Lamb of God to be sacrificed for the sins of the world (see John 1:29). This was the price he paid in order to bring glory to God and peace to those who would believe in him.

Pray

Thank you, Lord, that everyone is important to you—even poor, simple shepherds. Thank you that no matter how rich, smart, or important I am or am not, you came to save me from my sins. In Jesus's name, Amen.

Sing—*Once Again My Heart Rejoices* (p. 185)

> All my heart this night rejoices
> As I hear, far and near,
> Sweetest angel voices;
> "Christ is born," their choirs are singing,
> Till the air everywhere
> Now with joy is ringing.

Do

Place the symbol of the angel on your Advent tree.

Further Study for Adults

Notice the repetition of the word "glory." Add these verses to your word study on glory. Think about the light and the darkness in this scene. How did the shepherds react to the glory of the Lord? What did the angel say to reassure them? Are there areas of darkness in your life that you are afraid to expose to the light?

December 22
Jesus—Born of the Virgin Mary

When our son Mark was born, I couldn't wait to tell my friend Linda. Sure enough, as I expected, she was ecstatic! "I'll be right over!" she exclaimed when I phoned her from my hospital room. "But it's not visiting hours until six o'clock tonight!" I protested. "Never mind about that. I'll just sneak in," she said. Soon Linda's face was peering around my hospital door. She crept in and made a beeline for the bassinet in which Mark lay sleeping peacefully. Unfortunately, she hadn't been in my room long before a nurse came in and gave her a stern lecture. The fact that Linda was a nurse at another hospital didn't seem to matter to my grumpy nurse.

Linda's excitement and her desire to hurry over to the hospital to see my new baby and me demonstrated in her own special way that we were important to her.

After the angels disappeared, the shepherds didn't just say, "Wasn't that a nice concert?" and go about their business tending their flocks. They were excited! Let's see what they did.

Read—*Luke 2:15–20*

When the angels had left them and gone into heaven, the shepherds said to one another, "Let's go to Bethlehem and see this thing that has happened, which the Lord has told us about."

So they hurried off and found Mary and Joseph, and the baby, who was lying in the manger. When they had seen him, they spread the word concerning what had been told them about this child, and all who heard it were amazed at what the shepherds said to them. But Mary treasured up all these things and pondered them in her heart. The shepherds returned, glorifying and praising God for all the things they had heard and seen, which were just as they had been told.

Discuss
1. What did the shepherds want to do?
2. What did they do after they saw Jesus?

3. If you have asked Jesus to be your Savior, you too have met Jesus and you see him each day as you read his Word, the Bible. Do you get excited about him?

4. Whom can you tell about Jesus this week?

Final Thought

Good news is worth treasuring and telling. Just as Mary treasured these things in her heart, we need to spend time thinking about God and his work in our lives. Does Jesus make a difference in our lives? Then, like the shepherds, we must tell others so that they too may know Christ.

Pray

Thank you, Lord, that we can see you and worship you, just as the shepherds did. Help me to be excited about knowing you. Help me to tell my friends about all the good you have done. In Jesus's name, Amen.

Sing—*Away in a Manger* (p. 188)

> Away in a manger, no crib for his bed,
> The little Lord Jesus laid down his sweet head;
> The stars in the sky looked down where he lay,
> The little Lord Jesus, asleep on the hay.

Do

Find the symbol of the musical notes. Place this symbol on your Advent tree.

Further Study for Adults

What truths have you learned this Advent season that you have treasured in your heart? With whom can you share these things?

December 23
Jesus—Born of the Virgin Mary

Have you ever lost something important? One day I was putting away groceries and felt something scratch my hand. Looking down, I saw that the diamond was missing from my engagement ring. There were the four prongs with a big empty spot in the middle! I had absolutely no idea when it had fallen out. Where should I look? Carefully, I swept the kitchen floor, finding nothing but dirt. Then, on my hands and knees I searched the carpet. Finally I gave up. With sorrow I had to admit that my diamond was lost.

Today's passage is about some people who were searching for something—a newborn king. And it seems that they had lost something as well—a star.

Read—*Matthew 2:1–8*

After Jesus was born in Bethlehem in Judea, during the time of King Herod, Magi from the east came to Jerusalem and asked, "Where is the one who has been born king of the Jews? We saw his star in the east and have come to worship him."

When King Herod heard this he was disturbed, and all Jerusalem with him. When he had called together all the people's chief priests and teachers of the law, he asked them where the Christ was to be born. "In Bethlehem in Judea," they replied, "for this is what the prophet has written:

'But you, Bethlehem, in the land of Judah,
are by no means least among the rulers of Judah;
for out of you will come a ruler
who will be the shepherd of my people Israel.'"

Then Herod called the Magi secretly and found out from them the exact time the star had appeared. He sent them to Bethlehem and said, "Go and make a careful search for the child. As soon as you find him, report to me, so that I too may go and worship him."

Discuss

1. Why were the wise men looking for the newborn king?
2. Herod was a very wicked man who was the king of the Jews at that time. Why did he want to find Jesus?
3. Herod and the Magi were people of high position in their countries. Both wanted to find the Christ child. How were their motives different?
4. How did the people of Jerusalem respond to the Magi? Why?

Final Thought

For people who want to be in charge of their own lives, the message of Jesus seems like bad news, not good news. Jesus is not willing to fit comfortably into a neat little corner of our lives. He comes as King, or he does not come at all.

Pray

Dear Lord, I want to be like the wise men. They looked for you so that they could worship you. Help me to do this each day. In Jesus's name, Amen.

Sing—As With Gladness Men of Old (p. 189)

As with gladness men of old,
Did the guiding star behold;
As with joy they hailed its light,
Leading onward, beaming bright;
So, most gracious Lord may we
Ever more be led by thee.

Do

Place the symbol of the star on your Advent tree.

Further Study for Adults

Reflect on how Christ has met you and your family during this Advent season.

December 24
Jesus—Born of the Virgin Mary

If your family is like ours, excitement is at a fever-pitch by now. There are so many things we love about our family Christmas celebration. We set up a table in the family room in front of the fireplace, and there we eat special meals next to a blazing fire, with the lights of the Christmas tree brightening the room. The Christmas Eve service at church is always a highlight. Our hearts are lifted up in worship as we sing the beautiful Christmas hymns and listen to the choir and orchestra. God seems to speak directly to us through the words of the Holy Scripture and sermon.

For weeks, we have planned, sneaked, shopped, wrapped, and waited for this moment. I can't wait to see the looks on Mark's and Laura's faces when they see what we have given them. So far I have never been disappointed. They have always been utterly delighted and overflowing with appreciation.

In today's passage, we read about the giving of gifts. Remember that this does not take place on the night of Christ's birth. It happened sometime after his birth (see Matt. 2:1). By this time, Mary and Joseph were in a house (v. 11). But we do know that Jesus was less than two years old.

Read—*Matthew 2:9–12*

> After they had heard the king, they went on their way, and the star they had seen in the east went ahead of them until it stopped over the place where the child was. When they saw the star, they were overjoyed. On coming to the house, they saw the child with his mother Mary, and they bowed down and worshiped him. Then they opened their treasures and presented him with gifts of gold and of incense and of myrrh. And having been warned in a dream not to go back to Herod, they returned to their country by another route.

Discuss

1. How did the Magi feel when the star appeared again?

2. What did they do when they saw the child?
3. Why did they bring gifts? What does this tell us about the Magi?
4. What gift can you give to Jesus tonight?

Final Thought

Each of the gifts that the wise men brought has a special meaning. Gold stood for the riches of a king. Jesus would be King of kings. Incense was used by priests in temple worship. Jesus would be our high priest who would go between us and the Father. Myrrh was a perfume put on dead people. Jesus would die as the perfect sacrifice for our sins. The wise men's gifts showed that Jesus would be King, Priest, and Sacrifice.

Pray

Dear Lord, you gave your life for me. Nothing I could give you could ever repay you, but I know that you want me to give you my life. Lord, all that I am and have is yours. In Jesus's name, Amen.

Sing—*As With Gladness Men of Old* (p. 189)

As they offered gifts most rare,
At thy cradle, rude and bare,
So may we with holy joy,
Pure and free from sin's alloy
All our costliest treasures bring,
Christ, to thee, our heavenly king.

Do

Place the symbol of the wise men's gifts on your Advent tree.

Further Study for Adults

Thank God for all the gifts and blessings he has given you. Offer him your heart—every corner of it, for Christmas and for always.

Advent Devotions Year Two

The devotions for this second year of family celebrations at Advent center on the theme of Christ's coming.

These include:

❄ December 1–7
Promises of His Coming

❄ December 8–13
Preparation for His Coming

❄ December 14–17
Signs of His Coming

❄ December 18–24
Responses to His Coming

December 1
Promises of His Coming

Have you ever wanted to talk to an animal in its own language? My son Mark spends lots of time watching his pet goldfish Scooter, taking care of him, and even talking to him. Scooter seems to get excited when he hears Mark's voice. He "scoots" around his fish tank even faster! Though Mark can imagine what life is like for his fish, how much does Scooter understand about Mark? Not much, probably. The only way Mark could really communicate with Scooter would be for him to become a goldfish.

From the beginning of time, God has wanted men, women, and children to know him. But because he is so much greater than we are, there were limits to our understanding of him. The miracle of Christmas is that God put on human flesh so that he could show us what he is like in a way that we could understand!

Read—*Hebrews 1:1–3*

In the past God spoke to our forefathers through the prophets at many times and in various ways, but in these last days he has spoken to us by his Son, whom he appointed heir of all things, and through whom he made the universe. The Son is the radiance of God's glory and the exact representation of his being, sustaining all things by his powerful word. After he had provided purification for sins, he sat down at the right hand of the Majesty in heaven.

Discuss

1. These verses say that in the past God spoke to people through the prophets "at many times and in various ways." Can you remember some of the ways God spoke to the children of Israel in the Old Testament? (One of the most unusual ways was through a talking donkey! See Num. 22:21–31.)
2. How has God spoken to us "in these last days"?

3. What does it mean that Jesus is "the radiance of God's glory and the exact representation of his being?"
4. What else do we learn about Jesus in these verses?

Final Thought

While I am fond of Scooter, I don't love him enough to send my son to become a goldfish. Yet God did something very much like that!

Pray

Heavenly Father, thank you for loving us so much that you became one of us so that we could know you. Help us to pay careful attention to what you showed us about yourself. In the name of Jesus, who is the radiance of your glory, Amen.

Sing—*Oh, Come, All Ye Faithful* (p. 184)

Yea, Lord, we greet thee,
Born this happy morning,
Jesus, to thee be glory given;
Word of the Father,
Now in flesh appearing:

Oh, come, let us adore him,
Christ, the Lord!

Do

Find the symbol of the goldfish. Hang it on your Jesse tree.

Further Study for Adults

Begin a notebook or journal of your own Advent meditations. For your first entry, reflect on Hebrews 1:1–3. Always start with the facts: What does this passage say? Write down all the verbs (words of action or being) in this passage. Which ones refer to the Father? The Son? What do these verbs show us about God's character? How should we respond?

December 2
Promises of His Coming

Last summer, while camping in the mountains, I had to walk back to our campsite from the restroom in the dark—without a flashlight. Tall, shadowy trees on either side of the road shut out the starry sky. It was pitch dark. I could not see a thing, including my feet or the road. The funny thing was, I had no idea whether or not I was walking in the right direction. At times, I felt as though I were veering to one side of the road and I was afraid that I would step into a hole or fall into a ditch. I would correct my direction and veer in the other direction. The effect was that I zigged and zagged from one side of the road to another like a drunken sailor!

Isn't that what life would be like without Jesus, who is the Light of the World? In the darkness of sin, we weave from one direction to another, fearing that we will fall into a ditch. Without the light of Jesus, we have no idea whether we are walking straight (pleasing God) or veering off the road (heading for destruction).

Read—*Isaiah 9:2*

> The people walking in darkness
> have seen a great light;
> on those living in the land of the shadow of death
> a light has dawned.

Discuss

1. Have you ever been afraid of the dark?
2. Why is the darkness so scary?
3. Why do you think the Bible so often associates darkness with evil?
4. How has Jesus driven out darkness in the world? How has he driven out darkness in your life?

Final Thought

How comforting it was for me to see our tent in the distance, illuminated from the inside by a gas lantern so that the whole tent shone forth like a glowing, golden light against the darkness. So Jesus is both our light and our dwelling place. In him, we are safe for eternity!

Pray

Dear Lord Jesus, thank you that you came to bring light and hope into the world. Only in you can we live in safety. In your name, Amen.

Sing—*Silent Night* (p. 181)

> Silent night, holy night,
> Son of God, love's pure light
> Radiant beams from thy holy face,
> With the dawn of redeeming grace,
> Jesus, Lord, at thy birth.

Do

Find the symbol of the candle. Hang this on your Jesse tree.

Further Study for Adults

Read John 8:12. When Jesus spoke to the people, he said, "I am the light of the world. Whoever follows me will never walk in darkness, but will have the light of life." What does this mean?

December 3
Promises of His Coming

Try to imagine what it would be like if there were no Christmas. What would you miss the most? Now try to imagine what life would be like if Jesus had not come. How would your life be different? How would the world be different? There are many people, even in our own country, who have neither Christmas nor Jesus.

Perhaps this realization helps you to have a better feel for what it was like for people before Jesus came to earth. Most people worshiped other gods—angry, mean, horrible gods whom the people feared. If you have ever been afraid of someone, you know what a terrible thing fear is. It turns your stomach into a large knot and takes all the joy out of life.

For God's people, the Israelites, it was different. They had hope because of God's promises.

Read—*Isaiah 9:6*

> For to us a child is born,
> to us a son is given,
> and the government will be on his shoulders.
> And he will be called
> Wonderful Counselor, Mighty God
> Everlasting Father, Prince of Peace.

Discuss

1. Tell about a time when you were lost or in a situation where you were very frightened. Who helped you feel safe again?
2. Many children live in darkness and fear. Some don't have parents who love them and protect them. Some live in the middle of shootings and bombings. Still others live in countries where bad men are the rulers, and they don't care if the people are hungry or hurting. How would you feel if you were one of those children?

3. What hope do these verses offer?
4. How does Jesus fulfill this promise? Which of these titles best describes Jesus's role in your life at present?

Final Thought

The baby born in Bethlehem was in fact the Mighty God who came to earth to restore a right relationship between humanity and God.

Pray

Lord Jesus Christ, thank you for being our Wonderful Counselor, our Mighty God, our Everlasting Father, and our Prince of Peace. Help us to worship, serve, love, and obey you with our whole heart through all our days. Amen.

Sing—*Joy to the World* (p. 178)

> No more let sins and sorrows grow
> Nor thorns infest the ground;
> He comes to make his blessings flow
> Far as the curse is found.
> He rules the world with truth and grace,
> And makes the nations prove
> The glories of his righteousness,
> And wonders of his love.

Do

Find the symbol of the crown. Hang this on your Jesse tree.

Further Study for Adults

Look up these verses to see how Jesus is the fulfillment of the Isaiah 9:6 prophecy:

- Wonderful Counselor: John 14:16–18
- Mighty God: Titus 2:13
- Everlasting Father: John 10:30, John 8:23, 58
- Prince of Peace: Acts 5:31, 10:36

December 4
Promises of His Coming

Have you ever gone for a very long time without taking a bath? Once our family went on a camping trip where we were unable to shower or bathe for two weeks. Every morning I took a pan and a washcloth to the rest room. The water from the faucets in the sinks was ice cold. I washed my hair in the sink (brrr!), then filled the pan up and took it into one of the stalls and washed myself. This arrangement worked well but after a week or so, I was filled with a desperate urge to immerse myself in water. How I longed for a nice hot shower!

God uses the picture of a cleansing fountain (the ancient equivalent of a shower) to describe the savior he would send. When God spoke to his people through his prophets, or messengers, he often used pictures like this to help people understand his message in a practical way that related to their own everyday experience.

Read—*Zechariah 12:10, 13:1*

And I will pour out on the house of David and the inhabitants of Jerusalem a spirit of grace and supplication. They will look on me, the one they have pierced, and they will mourn for him as one mourns for an only child, and grieve bitterly for him as one grieves for a first-born son . . .

On that day a fountain will be opened to the house of David and the inhabitants of Jerusalem, to cleanse them from sin and impurity.

Discuss

1. God promised to open a fountain. How was that fountain to be used?
2. How is sin like dirt? When you have done something you know is wrong, like tell a lie, do you ever feel like

something inside you is dirty? Has Jesus cleansed you from your sin?

3. What else do these verses from Zechariah promise about the one that God would send (the Messiah)?

4. When you think about the fact that God himself came to earth to die so that we might be cleansed, how do you want to respond?

Final Thought

When we think about Christmas, often we forget that Jesus was born in order to die. His primary reason in coming was to die in our place. He needed to shed his blood on the cross—his blood is the fountain that cleanses us from sin and makes us able to live with God forever.

Pray

Thank you, Lord Jesus, that you came to earth in order to die for me. Thank you that your blood is the fountain that cleanses me of all my sin. I ask you to cleanse me now and make me yours forever. Amen.

Sing—O Lord, How Shall I Meet You (p. 177)

> Love caused your incarnation;
> Love brought you down to me.
> Your thirst for my salvation
> Procured my liberty.
> Oh, love beyond all telling
> That led thee to embrace
> In love, all love excelling,
> Our lost and fallen race.

Do

Find the symbol of the fountain. Hang this on your Jesse tree.

Further Study for Adults

Look up Hebrews 9:14, 22, 28. What do these verses tell us about blood and sin? About Christ's sacrifice? Now read Simeon's words to Mary in Luke 2:34–35. How do you suppose Mary felt when she heard this? How do these passages help you see Christmas in a different light?

December 5
Promises of His Coming

Do you remember the last time you were sick? Perhaps it was a cold or the flu, or perhaps it was some much more serious illness. We hardly ever think about being sick when we are well, but no one likes to feel awful—especially in the middle of the night. There is something terrible about being awake and miserable in the darkness and silence of the night. "If only morning would come!" you cry. Think about these feelings as you read these words from Malachi, the last prophet of the Old Testament.

Read—*Malachi 4:2*

But for you who revere my name, the sun of righteousness will rise with healing in its wings. And you will go out and leap like calves released from the stall.

Discuss

1. When the sun of righteousness rises, what will it have in its wings?
2. What does this verse say will happen?
3. To whom is this promise given? What does it mean to "revere my name"?
4. Read Luke 1:78–79 to see how this prophecy is fulfilled. This was part of the song of praise of Zechariah, the father of John the Baptist. He was talking about John's mission, to prepare the way for the "rising sun from heaven." Who was that?

Final Thought

I feel like that when I am finally well after being sick. Sin in our lives is the worst kind of sickness. It eats away at our hearts. It paralyzes us and keeps us from having the energy to do all the good things that God made us to do. When the light of Jesus comes into our lives, he heals us from the terrible disease of sin. He brings us joy, life, strength, and release.

Pray

Thank you so much, Lord Jesus, that you came to bring healing to our hearts and lives. Thank you for releasing me from the disease of sin and giving me new life and strength. Amen.

Sing—*Hark! The Herald Angels Sing* (p. 180)

Hail, the heaven-born Prince of Peace!
Hail, the Sun of Righteousness!
Light and life to all he brings,
Risen with healing in his wings.
Mild he lays his glory by,
Born that man no more may die,
Born to raise the sons of earth,
Born to give them second birth.
Hark! The herald angels sing,
"Glory to the newborn King!"

Do

Find the symbol of the sun with wings. Hang it on your Jesse tree.

Further Study for Adults

Read Isaiah 53:4–6. What does this passage say about our need? What words are used to describe what the Messiah would go through in order to meet our need? Are there sins or hurts in your life that need the healing touch of the "sun of righteousness"? Write a prayer offering these to Christ.

December 6
Promises of His Coming

Gift-giving has become a big part of our Christmas celebrations—too big, parents might agree. By now you have probably made out your Christmas list—or else you have been letting your family know what you want as things occur to you. (With catalogs and sales flyers streaming in through the mail every day, it's hard not to get ideas for new things that you would like to have.)

What did you get for Christmas last year? Are you as excited about these things now as you were then? Perhaps some of your gifts have broken, or parts are missing. Some are used up, and several lie forgotten on a shelf. No matter how much we want something, in the end, it just cannot satisfy us forever.

People all over the world and throughout the ages have had wants or desires, yet rarely are people satisfied when they get what they want. Perhaps that is because what we think we want is different from what our heart truly desires.

Read—*Haggai 2:7*

I will shake all nations, and the desired of all nations will come, and I will fill this house with glory, says the LORD Almighty.

Discuss

1. This is another promise that God gave to his people through one of his prophets. What did he say will come (to Israel)?

2. What does God say he will do when the "desired of all nations" comes?

3. Remember how in the days of Moses and the Exodus, God's glory filled the tabernacle in the cloud? Read Exodus 40:34–35. Why do you suppose Moses could not enter?

4. The glory of God is evident when he makes his presence known. This prophecy from Haggai would be fulfilled in Jesus, who is the presence of God in human form. How did Jesus's first coming fulfill this prophecy?

Final Thought

The deepest need and longing of every human heart, the world over, can only be satisfied, fully and forever, in Jesus Christ. He is the presence and glory of God. He came that we might have life, and have it to the full (John 10:10).

Sing—*Angels from the Realms of Glory* (p. 190)

> Sages, leave your contemplations,
> Brighter visions beam afar;
> Seek the great Desire of nations,
> You have seen his natal star;
> Come and worship, come and worship,
> Worship Christ, the newborn King.

Do

Find the symbol of the flags. This refers to the nations that would come to him and find their desires met in Christ. Hang this symbol on your Jesse tree.

Further Study for Adults

Read Isaiah 60:1–3, 9, 18–22. What do these verses tell us about the Lord's coming? Make a list, putting in your own words facts about his coming found in this passage. How were these prophecies fulfilled in Christ's first coming? How might they be fulfilled in his second coming? How have they been fulfilled in your life?

December 7
Promises of His Coming

As I write this, preparations are being made for the inauguration of our newly elected president. Because we live just outside Washington, DC, we hear more about it than people in many parts of the country. Area public schools have declared January 20 a holiday so that the children are free to go watch the parade. Like a monumental wedding, this event is being anticipated with much careful planning, hard work, and excitement.

Many people are wondering what kind of leader our new president will be. How will our families, our economy, and our country's involvement in the world be affected by his decisions? At the time of this writing, it is still all speculation.

Once again, we turn to Isaiah to look at promises of the coming Savior. How much more exciting than a presidential inauguration is the thought of getting ready for the inauguration of the King of kings! These verses tell about what kind of a ruler he will be.

Read—*Isaiah 11:4–5*

> But with righteousness he will judge the needy,
> with justice he will give decisions for the poor of the
>   earth.
> He will strike the earth with the rod of his mouth;
> with the breath of his lips he will slay the wicked.
> Righteousness will be his belt
> and faithfulness the sash around his waist.

Discuss

1. Have you ever said, "That's not fair!"? What does it feel like when a grown-up isn't fair to you?

2. These verses point to the day that Jesus comes again to rule the earth. What kind of king will he be?
3. What do these verses say will be Jesus's weapon against evil?
4. Describe in your own words the characteristics of Christ's rulership. How will this change our world? How does his rulership affect your life now?

Final Thought

We long for the day when all wrongs are righted, the poor and needy are cared for, and the wicked get their just desserts. Come quickly, Lord Jesus!

Sing—*Joy to the World* (p. 178)

Joy to the world! The Lord is come;
Let earth receive her King;
Let every heart prepare him room,
And heaven and nature sing.

He rules the world with truth and grace,
And makes the nations prove
The glories of his righteousness,
And wonders of his love.

Pray

Dear Lord, we are so glad that you are a good ruler who sets things right. Thank you for setting things right in our hearts and our relationship with God. And we look forward to the day when you will come again to set things right in the world. In Jesus's name, Amen.

Do

Find the symbol of the gavel. This reminds us that Jesus is the righteous judge. Hang this on your Jesse tree.

Further Study for Adults

What changes do you most desire when you anticipate Christ's rule on this earth? Write out each phrase of Isaiah 11:4–5 in your own words. Is Christ ruling in your life? Can your life better reflect his kingship?

December 8
Preparation for His Coming

Do you enjoy having company? What preparations do you make when special friends are coming for dinner, or loved ones are arriving from out of town? I enjoy planning the menu and preparing a special meal. Then there is the housecleaning, not as much fun to do, but when everyone pitches in, it's not so difficult. Finally, there comes the moment when the guests arrive. Our dog usually ensures that they are welcomed at the door with great enthusiasm. Smiles, hugs, and warm greetings are exchanged. (The dog needs to be calmed down.) So begins a wonderful evening of fellowship with people we love.

God's prophet Isaiah tells about the arrival of someone very special and the preparations that need to be made.

Read—*Isaiah 62:10–12*

>Pass through, pass through the gates!
>Prepare the way for the people.
>Build up, build up the highway!
>Remove the stones.
>Raise a banner for the nations.
>
>The LORD has made proclamation
>to the ends of the earth:
>"Say to the Daughter of Zion,
>'See, your Savior comes!
>See, his reward is with him,
>and his recompense accompanies him.'"
>They will be called the Holy People,
>the Redeemed of the LORD;
>and you will be called Sought After,
>the City No Longer Deserted.

Discuss

1. What are some of the ways people are to prepare for the Savior?
2. Advent is a time, not only to prepare for celebrating Jesus's birth, but also to prepare our hearts for Jesus's second coming. How?
3. Jesus comes ushering in a new community, with a new identity. What are the four names which identify his people? What does each name mean?
4. If Jesus were to return today, would you be ready? What areas might you want to get in order?

Final Thought

Those who love the Lord need not fear his coming. We look forward to that day with joy. It will be more wonderful than we can imagine.

Sing—*Good Christian Friends, Rejoice* (p. 183)

Good Christian friends rejoice, With heart and soul and voice;
Now ye hear of endless bliss: Jesus Christ was born for this!
He has opened heaven's door, And we are blest forevermore.
Christ was born for this! Christ was born for this!

Pray

Dear Lord Jesus, I open wide the gates of my heart. Help me to prepare with joy for your coming. In your Holy Name, Amen.

Do

Find the symbol of the gate. Hang this on your Jesse tree.

Further Study for Adults

Reflect on how Christ's coming into your life has changed your identity. How do the four names of verse 12 apply to you?

December 9
Preparation for His Coming

Have you ever been driving in the car and realized that you were going in the wrong direction? Do you continue in the same direction, even though you know that where you want to go is the opposite way? John the Baptist came to prepare the way for Jesus's ministry, and he called the people to repentance. When the people were baptized in the Jordan River, they were saying, "I've been going in the wrong direction. From now on, I'm going to go in God's direction."

Read—*Mark 1:2–8*

It is written in Isaiah the prophet:

"I will send my messenger ahead of you,
who will prepare your way"—
"a voice of one calling in the desert,
'Prepare the way for the Lord,
Make straight paths for him.'"

And so John came, baptizing in the desert region and preaching a baptism of repentance for the forgiveness of sins. The whole Judean countryside and all the people of Jerusalem went out to him. Confessing their sins, they were baptized by him in the Jordan River. John wore clothing made of camel's hair, with a leather belt around his waist, and he ate locusts and wild honey. And this was his message: "After me will come one more powerful than I, the thongs of whose sandals I am not worthy to stoop down and untie. I baptize you with water, but he will baptize you with the Holy Spirit."

Discuss

1. What did John look like? What kind of a person do you think he was?

2. What was John's job? Who gave him this job? (Look at Mark 1:2–3 to find out.)
3. Put John's message in your own words. Why do you think God sent him with this message at that particular time?
4. How would Jesus's ministry be different from John's (v. 8)?

Final Thought

Advent is a time to prepare for Christ's coming by looking at our lives and seeing if there are habits, attitudes, or behaviors of which we need to repent. But these changes are so much more difficult than making a U-turn in a car! In fact, the kinds of changes that God requires are impossible for us to make. Only when Jesus comes into our lives by the power of the Holy Spirit is true transformation possible.

Pray

Dear Lord, there are things that need to change in my life. Please change me to be like Jesus. Only you can do it through your Holy Spirit. Help me to cooperate with your Spirit by listening to you and obeying you. In Jesus's name, Amen.

Sing—*Oh, Come, Oh, Come, Emmanuel* (p. 176)

> Oh, come, Oh, come, Emmanuel,
> And ransom captive Israel;
> That mourns in lonely exile here,
> Until the Son of God appear.
> Rejoice! Rejoice! Emmanuel
> Shall come to thee, O Israel.

Do

Find the symbol of the highway in the wilderness. Hang this on your Jesse tree.

Further Study for Adults

Read Galatians 5:22–26. Think about your relationships at home, work, church, and in your neighborhood. Do your relationships exhibit these characteristics? What attitudes and behaviors in your life need to change?

December 10
Preparation for His Coming

Today as I was walking with my friend Martha, we came upon a crowd gathered along the west side of the overpass spanning I-66, the interstate that goes from the Shenandoah Mountains through northern Virginia into Washington, DC. I walk this way often, but I have never seen a crowd gathered. There was even a police officer there. "What's going on?" I asked someone. "It's the president-elect's motorcade," they told me.

I peered over shoulders and through the chain-link fence down at the deserted highway below. Sure enough, within minutes a police helicopter flew overhead and several police cars raced eastward.

"Here they come!" someone shouted. Dozens of police motorcycles rounded the bend, followed by bus after bus after bus, lights on. As they approached our bridge, we all waved. The traffic going the opposite direction slowed down and pulled over to watch the president-elect arrive in Washington officially for the first time.

As Martha and I continued on with our walk, we marveled at our good fortune. The crowd had been watching and waiting for an hour. We just happened to be walking by at the right moment. On our way home, we saw another crowd, a smaller one this time, gathered at the bridge. We sadly informed them that they had missed the big event. The president had come earlier than expected.

Jesus told a story about watching and waiting.

Read—*Matthew 24:42–44*

Therefore keep watch, because you do not know on what day your Lord will come. But understand this: If the owner of the house had known at what time of night the thief was coming, he would have kept watch and would not have let his house be broken into. So you also must be ready, because the Son of Man will come at an hour when you do not expect him.

Discuss

1. Who are the characters in Jesus's story?
2. What happened?
3. How is Jesus like a thief?
4. Why does Jesus tell this story? What can we do to be ready for his coming?

Final Thought

Jesus is not a bad man, like a thief, whose coming we need to fear. And he is a million times greater than the president of the United States. Let's watch for his coming with excitement and joy! That day will be better than all the Christmases and birthdays of your life rolled into one!

Pray

Dear Lord Jesus, help us to be ready for your coming and not to be caught by surprise like the owner of the house in Jesus's story. We want to be watching and waiting with joy. In your name, Amen.

Sing—*O Lord, How Shall I Meet You* (p. 177)

O Lord how shall I meet you, How welcome you aright?
Your people long to greet you, My Hope, my heart's
delight!
O kindle, Lord most holy, Thy lamp within my breast,
To do in spirit lowly, All that may please thee best.

Do

Find the symbol of the house. Hang this on your Jesse tree.

Further Study for Adults

Read Matthew 24:45–51 and 25:1–13. How are these two parables similar? How are they different? With which of the characters in these stories can you most closely identify? What is God's message to you personally regarding readiness?

December 11
Preparation for His Coming

We have been looking at what we should do to prepare for Jesus's coming. Now for the next three days, we will continue the same theme, but we will look at three people who prepared for the coming of Jesus. The first of these three people is Mary, the mother of Jesus.

Read—*Luke 1:26–38*

In the sixth month, God sent the angel Gabriel to Nazareth, a town in Galilee, to a virgin pledged to be married to a man named Joseph, a descendant of David. The virgin's name was Mary. The angel went to her and said, "Greetings, you who are highly favored! The Lord is with you."

Mary was greatly troubled at his words and wondered what kind of greeting this might be. But the angel said to her, "Do not be afraid, Mary, you have found favor with God. You will be with child and give birth to a son, and you are to give him the name Jesus. He will be great and will be called the Son of the Most High. The Lord God will give him the throne of his father David, and he will reign over the house of Jacob forever; his kingdom will never end."

"How will this be," Mary asked the angel, "since I am a virgin?"

The angel answered, "The Holy Spirit will come upon you, and the power of the Most High will overshadow you. So the holy one to be born will be called the Son of God. Even Elizabeth your relative is going to have a child in her old age, and she who was said to be barren is in her sixth month. For nothing is impossible with God."

"I am the Lord's servant," Mary answered. "May it be to me as you have said." Then the angel left her.

Discuss

1. How did the angel Gabriel greet Mary?
2. What does Luke say were Mary's thoughts and feelings?

3. From these verses, what do we know about Mary?
4. What was her final answer to the angel? Are there areas of your life in which you need to give that answer to Christ?

Final Thought

Mary was probably very young, between thirteen and sixteen years old. No matter how young or old we are, the very best way to prepare for Jesus's coming is to give ourselves to him as Mary did.

Pray

Dear Lord, sometimes I am troubled at your words, just as Mary was. Help me, like Mary, simply to give myself to you. Do your work in my life, I pray, in Jesus's name, Amen.

Sing—*Away in a Manger* (p. 188)

Be near me, Lord Jesus; I ask you to stay
Close by me forever and love me, I pray.
Bless all the dear children in your tender care
And fit us for heaven to live with you there.

Do

Find the symbol of the angel. Hang this on your Jesse tree.

Further Study for Adults

Read Mary's song of praise to God, recorded in Luke 1:46–55. This song is a compilation of Scripture verses. If you have a study or reference Bible, look up some of the references listed in the margin. What does this song tell you about Mary's spiritual life and training? What steps can you take to enhance your own spiritual life and training so that Scripture flows out of you as it did Mary? If you are a parent, how can you guide your children in these matters?

December 12
Preparation for His Coming

Yesterday we saw how Mary gave herself to the Lord in preparation for his coming. The next thing she did was take a trip to visit a relative. Why do you suppose she did that?

Read—*Luke 1:39–45*

> At that time Mary got ready and hurried to a town in the hill country of Judea, where she entered Zechariah's home and greeted Elizabeth. When Elizabeth heard Mary's greeting, the baby leaped in her womb, and Elizabeth was filled with the Holy Spirit. In a loud voice she exclaimed: "Blessed are you among women, and blessed is the child you will bear! But why am I so favored, that the mother of my Lord should come to me? As soon as the sound of your greeting reached my ears, the baby in my womb leaped for joy. Blessed is she who has believed that what the Lord has said to her will be accomplished!"

Discuss

1. When you are excited about going somewhere, do you get ready slowly, or do you hurry? Which did Mary do?
2. What happened to Elizabeth when Mary said hello?
3. Mary was very young and Elizabeth was very old. But they had several very important things in common. What were they?
4. Why do you think Mary was so eager to be with her relative Elizabeth? How did Elizabeth (and her baby, who was John the Baptist) help Mary to prepare for Jesus's coming?

Final Thought

When God does something wonderful in our lives, we always like to have a Christian friend or family member with whom we can share the experience. If they are discouraged, our words will serve as encouragement to them. They can understand and share our excitement. Then later, when we are discouraged, they can remind us of God's goodness to us.

Pray

Dear Lord Jesus, thank you for the Christian friends and family members you have given us. Help us to share with them the good things that you are doing in our lives. Help us also to lean on them when we need their encouragement. In Jesus's name, Amen.

Sing—*Once Again My Heart Rejoices* (p. 185)

Once again my heart rejoices
As I hear, far and near,
sweetest angel voices:
Christ is born, their choirs are singing,
Till the air everywhere
now with joy is ringing.

Come then, let us hasten yonder;
Here let all, great and small,
kneel in awe and wonder,
Love him who with love is yearning;
Hail the star that from far
bright with hope is burning.

Do

Find the symbol of the smiling face. This reminds us of the joy of Christian friendship. Hang this symbol on the Jesse tree.

Further Study for Adults

Read the entire account of Elizabeth and Zechariah found in Luke 1:5–25, 57–80. What do we learn about Elizabeth and Zechariah from these verses? How might Mary's visit have been a real help and encouragement to Elizabeth? Is there someone in your extended family or your church family who might be in need of special encouragement?

December 13
Preparation for His Coming

Do you remember your dreams? I find that if I don't tell someone my dream soon after I wake up, the dream fades away just as mist rising off a lake vanishes in the morning sunlight. Most of the time, I'm glad that my dream isn't real, aren't you? Here is an account of a very special dream—one that was real. Think about how Joseph felt as you read.

Read—*Matthew 1:18–25*

This is how the birth of Jesus Christ came about: His mother Mary was pledged to be married to Joseph, but before they came together, she was found to be with child through the Holy Spirit. Because Joseph her husband was a righteous man and did not want to expose her to public disgrace, he had in mind to divorce her quietly.

But after he had considered this, an angel of the Lord appeared to him in a dream and said, "Joseph son of David, do not be afraid to take Mary home as your wife, because what is conceived in her is from the Holy Spirit. She will give birth to a son, and you are to give him the name Jesus, because he will save his people from their sins."

All this took place to fulfill what the Lord had said through the prophet: "The virgin will be with child and will give birth to a son, and they will call him Immanuel"—which means, "God with us."

When Joseph woke up, he did what the angel of the Lord had commanded him and took Mary home as his wife. But he had no union with her until she gave birth to a son. And he gave him the name Jesus.

Discuss

1. Who was in Joseph's dream?
2. What was the message that he gave Joseph?

3. What kind of a person was Joseph?

4. How did Joseph prepare for the coming of the Savior?

Final Thought

Most likely, Joseph had never imagined that he would be the stepfather of the Messiah. Yet here comes the angel of the Lord, asking Joseph to believe something unbelievable! How do we know that Joseph believed the angel? Because "when Joseph woke up, he did what the angel of the Lord had commanded him."

Often God calls us to believe the unbelievable and do the impossible. How can we do this? We must simply take God at his word as Joseph did, and then immediately obey. If, every day, we listen to God's Word and obey it without hesitation, we, like Joseph, will be ready for his coming.

Pray

Dear Lord, open my ears and my heart to pay attention to your Word. Make my hands and feet ready to obey you quickly and cheerfully. In Jesus's name, Amen.

Sing—*All Glory, Laud, and Honor* (p. 187)

> All glory, laud and honor, to you redeemer, king
> To whom the lips of children made sweet hosannas ring.
> You are the king of Israel
> And David's royal Son,
> Now in the Lord's name coming,
> Our King and Blessed One.

Do

Find the symbol of the bed. Hang it on your Jesse tree.

Further Study for Adults

Read Matthew 1 and 2, listing all the unexpected changes and challenges that Joseph faced. How did he respond? What challenges are you facing?

December 14
Signs of His Coming

What are the signs of spring where you live? Flocks of robins gather in our yard, pecking the earth and gorging themselves on earthworms. Purple and yellow crocuses emerge from the ground and open like tiny teacups. Just like the coming of spring, the coming of the Savior, Jesus, was marked by certain special signs. We will be taking the next couple of days to look at these signs and how the Savior's birth was announced through them.

Read—*Micah 5:2; Luke 2:1–7*

But you, Bethlehem Ephrathah,
though you are small among the clans of Judah,
out of you will come for me
one who will be ruler over Israel,
whose origins are from of old,
from ancient times.

In those days Caesar Augustus issued a decree that a census should be taken of the entire Roman world. (This was the first census that took place while Quirinius was governor of Syria.) And everyone went to his own town to register.

So Joseph also went up from the town of Nazareth in Galilee to Judea, to Bethlehem the town of David, because he belonged to the house and line of David. He went there to register with Mary, who was pledged to be married to him and was expecting a child. While they were there, the time came for the baby to be born, and she gave birth to her firstborn, a son. She wrapped him in cloths and placed him in a manger, because there was no room for them in the inn.

Discuss

1. Where did Joseph and Mary live?
2. Why did he take Mary and go to Bethlehem?

3. The first verses we read were a promise God made hundreds of years earlier. What was his promise? How did he keep it?
4. How was Jesus's birth in Bethlehem a sign? What did it signify?

Final Thought

Even Caesar Augustus acted as God's instrument in orchestrating the birth of the Messiah in the prophesied Bethlehem. The taking of a census—is there anything more secular than that? Yet God uses the most seemingly "unspiritual" things to accomplish his purposes.

Pray

Dear Father, we're so glad that you are in charge of our world. We know that we can trust you to take care of us. Through Jesus Christ our Lord, Amen.

Sing—O *Little Town of Bethlehem* (p. 179)

O little town of Bethlehem,
How still we see thee lie!
Above thy deep and dreamless sleep
The silent stars go by;
Yet in thy dark streets shineth
The everlasting Light;
The hopes and fears of all the years
Are met in thee tonight.

Do

Hang the symbol of the Bethlehem building on your Jesse tree.

Further Study for Adults

Write in your own words the following verses: Proverbs 16:4, Ecclesiastes 7:14, and Romans 8:28. How is this a comfort to you?

December 15
Signs of His Coming

When you give someone directions to your house, what do you tell them to look for? Our house is easy to miss, so I tell people to look for the house with the blue shutters and the cedar shake roof. Those features make our house unique on our street, thereby making it easier to spot while driving by. As you read about the shepherds, think about the angel giving them directions to find Jesus. What were the landmarks they were to find in their search for the new baby?

Read—*Luke 2:8–14*

And there were shepherds living out in the fields nearby, keeping watch over their flocks at night. An angel of the Lord appeared to them, and the glory of the Lord shone around them, and they were terrified. But the angel said to them, "Do not be afraid. I bring you good news of great joy that will be for all the people. Today in the town of David a Savior has been born to you; he is Christ the Lord. This will be a sign to you: You will find a baby wrapped in cloths and lying in a manger."

Suddenly a great company of the heavenly host appeared with the angel, praising God and saying,

"Glory to God in the highest,
and on earth peace to men on whom his favor rests."

Discuss

1. How did the shepherds feel when the angel appeared?
2. What did the angels say? What were the shepherds supposed to look for?
3. There is more than one sign in these verses. What else was a sign to the shepherds that something extraordinary was taking place?
4. List all the things that the shepherds learned from the angels.

Final Thought

I'm so glad that God pays attention to details! He didn't send the shepherds off to Bethlehem without any clue as to where to look. And he is just as attentive to the details of our lives. If we want to follow him, he gives us signs along the way. The question is, are we looking?

Pray

Dear Lord, thank you that you gave signs to the shepherds and you give signs to us today. Keep our eyes open to see the signs that you give us. We want to follow you. In Jesus's name, Amen.

Sing—*Angels We Have Heard on High* (p. 182)

> Shepherds, why this jubilee?
> Why your joyous strains prolong?
> What the gladsome tidings be?
> Which inspire your heav'nly song?

> Gloria in excelsis Deo. Gloria in excelsis Deo.

Do

Find the symbol of the manger. Hang it on your Jesse tree.

Further Study for Adults

Look at the angels' messages. For whom is this good news? See verses 10, 11, and 14. To whom does God promise peace? Are these messages contradictory? Why or why not?

December 16
Signs of His Coming

While we are looking at the signs of Jesus's coming as a baby, we should also remember that Jesus is coming again. The next time Jesus comes, he will not come as a baby, but as King of kings and Lord of lords. When Jesus talked to his disciples about the special day when he would come again, he told them to watch for certain signs.

Read—*Matthew 24:3, 30–31*

As Jesus was sitting on the Mount of Olives, the disciples came to him privately. "Tell us," they said, "when will this happen, and what will be the sign of your coming and of the end of the age?"

Jesus answered . . . "At that time the sign of the Son of Man will appear in the sky, and all the nations of the earth will mourn. They will see the Son of Man coming on the clouds of the sky, with power and great glory. And he will send his angels with a loud trumpet call, and they will gather his elect from the four winds, from one end of the heavens to the other."

Discuss

1. What will be the signs of Jesus's coming?
2. Describe the picture you see in your mind when you hear these words of Jesus.
3. How will Jesus's second coming be like his first coming? How will it be different?
4. Why might the nations of the earth mourn? What will happen to those who love God, or "his elect"?

Final Thought

When we think about Jesus coming again in glory and power, we realize all that he gave up when he came to earth the first time. Only when he comes again will people realize what they have done by rejecting Jesus Christ. Let us not be of one those who reject him and then must mourn. Rather let us love him and be among those who are gathered together on that day!

Pray

Dear Lord Jesus Christ, we worship and adore you: the great King of kings. We look forward to your coming again in glory. Keep us alert so that we watch for the signs of your coming. In your name, Amen.

Sing—*Angels from the Realms of Glory* (p. 190)

> Angels from the realms of glory,
> Wing your flight o'er all the earth;
> Once you sang creation's story
> Now proclaim Messiah's birth:
>
> Come and worship,
> Come and worship,
> Worship Christ, the newborn king.

Do

Find the symbol of the trumpet. Hang it on your Jesse tree.

Further Study for Adults

Read Matthew 24:1–41. Write down all the signs of Jesus's coming revealed in these verses. What strikes you about this picture? Does this engender hope or fear in your heart? If Jesus came today, whom do you know and love who would not be "gathered together" with "his elect"? If you knew he were coming tomorrow, what would you do differently today?

December 17
Signs of His Coming

Do you know anyone who is from a different country? At my daughter Laura's school, there are students from fifty different nationalities. One of the boys in her class recently arrived from Taiwan. He speaks little English. Think how difficult it would be to be in a school where the teacher was speaking a language you didn't understand! For Fu-chun, so many things here are different and strange. Yet Fu-chun and I are brother and sister in Christ! Every day Fu-chun reads his Chinese Bible during lunch.

In Isaiah 60:3, God promised Jerusalem that "Nations will come to your light." When the promised Messiah came, he would draw men, women, and children from every nation. Fu-chun is one of those children, and so am I!

Remember how God gave the sign of the angels to the poor shepherds on the hillside near Bethlehem? God also gave a sign to some who were from a different country.

Read—*Matthew 2:1–2*

> After Jesus was born in Bethlehem in Judea, during the time of King Herod, Magi from the east came to Jerusalem and asked, "Where is the one who has been born king of the Jews? We saw his star in the east and have come to worship him."

Discuss

1. Magi were not kings, but were astrologers, or people who studied the positions of the stars. How many Magi were there? (If you said three, read the verses again!) What were they riding on? (If you said camels, look again!)
2. Did the Magi visit Jesus on the night of his birth? How do you know?

3. What do we know about these Magi? They probably came from what is now Iran and Saudi Arabia. What made them want to come to Jerusalem?
4. When they saw the sign of the star, what was their response?

Final Thought

The Magi were men from a culture who did not worship the one true God—yet they saw something in the sky that convinced them God had come to earth! They went to great expense and inconvenience to travel across the known world in orde r to see and worship this newborn King. Obviously God had made their hearts ready so that when they saw the sign of the star, they responded.

Pray

Dear Heavenly Father, thank you that Jesus came not only for the Jews but for people from every nationality. Help us to share your good news with people from every culture, so that those whose hearts are ready, like the Magi, will come to you. In Jesus's name, Amen.

Sing—*As With Gladness Men of Old* (p. 189)

As with joyful steps they sped,
Savior, to thy lowly bed,
There to bend the knee before
Thee, whom heav'n and earth adore;
So may we with willing feet
Ever seek thy mercy seat.

Do

Find the symbol of the star. Hang it on your Jesse tree.

Further Study for Adults

Reflect on the signposts that God used in your life to lead you to Christ. Perhaps God's signposts were people—parents, a Sunday school teacher, a friend. Perhaps God used times of difficulty or crisis to bring you into relationship with him.

December 18

Responses to His Coming

Yesterday we read about the Magi and the sign that God gave to them, the sign of the star. We also saw how they responded to that sign by coming to worship him. From now until Christmas, we will be looking at the many responses to Christ's coming.

Read—*Matthew 2:3–8, 12–15*

When King Herod heard this he was disturbed, and all Jerusalem with him. When he had called together all the people's chief priests and teachers of the law, he asked them where the Christ was to be born. "In Bethlehem in Judea," they replied, "for this is what the prophet has written:
    'But you, Bethlehem, in the land of Judah
    are by no means least among the rulers of Judah;
    for out of you will come a ruler
    who will be the shepherd of my people Israel.'"
    Then Herod called the Magi secretly and found out from them the exact time the star had appeared. He sent them to Bethlehem and said, "Go and make a careful search for the child. As soon as you find him, report to me, so that I too may go and worship him."
    . . . And having been warned in a dream not to go back to Herod, they returned to their country by another route.
    When they had gone, an angel of the Lord appeared to Joseph in a dream. "Get up," he said, "take the child and his mother and escape to Egypt. Stay there until I tell you, for Herod is going to search for the child to kill him."
    So he got up, took the child and his mother during the night and left for Egypt, where he stayed until the death of Herod. And so was fulfilled what the Lord had said through the prophet: "Out of Egypt I called my son."

Discuss

1. Was Herod happy to hear about a newborn king? Why not?
2. Was Herod going to worship Jesus? What was he planning?
3. Compare Herod's response with the response of the Magi.
4. Why do you think Herod reacted so violently?

Final Thought

When it comes right down to it, these are the only two possible responses to Jesus Christ. We either want to be kings ourselves, as Herod did, or we surrender to the King of kings. We crucify him or we worship him. There is no middle ground.

Pray

Dear Lord Jesus Christ, we want to be like the Magi, not like Herod. Please rule in our lives. In your precious name, Amen.

Sing—O *Little Town of Bethlehem* (p. 179)

How silently, how silently,
The wondrous gift is given!
So God imparts to human hearts
The blessings of his heaven.
No ear may hear his coming,
But in this world of sin,
Where meek souls will receive him, still
The dear Christ enters in.

Do

Find the symbol of the black heart. Hang it on your Jesse tree.

Further Study for Adults

Study the Matthew and Luke narratives, looking at all the different ways in which God spoke to various people concerning Christ. How does God speak to you?

December 19
Responses to His Coming

By now you have been waiting for Christmas for several weeks at least. Some of us have been waiting much longer than that! When I am excited about something happening, like Christmas, it seems to take forever! Waiting is one of the hardest things we do. Let's look at someone who waited many years for Jesus's birth.

Read—*Luke 2:25–35*

Now there was a man in Jerusalem called Simeon, who was righteous and devout. He was waiting for the consolation of Israel, and the Holy Spirit was upon him. It had been revealed to him by the Holy Spirit that he would not die before he had seen the Lord's Christ. Moved by the Spirit, he went into the temple courts. When the parents brought in the child Jesus to do for him what the custom of the Law required, Simeon took him in his arms and praised God, saying:

"Sovereign Lord, as you have promised,
you now dismiss your servant in peace.
For my eyes have seen your salvation,
which you have prepared in the sight of all people,
a light for revelation to the Gentiles
and for glory to your people Israel."

The child's father and mother marveled at what was said about him. Then Simeon blessed them and said to Mary, his mother: "This child is destined to cause the falling and rising of many in Israel, and to be a sign that will be spoken against, so that the thoughts of many hearts will be revealed. And a sword will pierce your own soul too."

Discuss

1. What was the promise that God had given to Simeon?
2. What did Simeon do when he saw Jesus?

3. What kind of a person was Simeon?

4. How did Simeon respond to seeing Jesus at last?

Final Thought

Sometimes when we wait a long time and look forward to something, we are disappointed when it arrives. It fails to meet our expectations. Not so with Jesus! Simeon found him more than worth the wait. Jesus will never, ever fail us. He always keeps his promises.

Pray

Dear Lord, we are so thankful that you do keep your promises and you never fail us. Give us the patience to wait for your answers just as Simeon did. In Jesus's name, Amen.

Sing—*Silent Night* (p. 181)

Silent night, holy night,
All is calm, all is bright
Round yon virgin mother and child.
Holy Infant, so tender and mild,
Sleep in heavenly peace.
Sleep in heavenly peace.

Do

Find the symbol of the eyes (from Simeon's song of praise). Hang it on your Jesse tree.

Further Study for Adults

Study Simeon's words to Mary. How were they fulfilled? How do you suppose Mary felt when she heard them?

December 20
Responses to His Coming

Whom do you know who is elderly and who has loved the Lord for many years? When I was a child, there was an old man in our church named Mr. Rowe. He was a gentle and humble man, and it was evident that he knew God. God's light seemed to radiate from his face. Everything he said and did was full of God's love. He did not speak often, but when he did, everyone listened.

Besides being a beloved member of our church, Mr. Rowe was our church custodian. He was always there, cleaning the floors, scrubbing the bathrooms, regulating the furnace, doing all the tasks that no one thinks about but expects to have done. He never complained but simply went about his tasks with the joy that comes from serving Christ. And when I saw him, I felt like I was in the presence of the Lord.

Today we look at another response to the baby Jesus—the response of an elderly woman who truly loved God.

Read—*Luke 2:36–38*

> There was also a prophetess, Anna, the daughter of Phanuel, of the tribe of Asher. She was very old; she had lived with her husband seven years after her marriage, and then was a widow until she was eighty-four. She never left the temple but worshiped night and day, fasting and praying. Coming up to them at that very moment she gave thanks to God and spoke about the child to all who were looking forward to the redemption of Jerusalem.

Discuss

1. How old was Anna?
2. What did Anna do all day?
3. Do you think it was a coincidence that Anna happened to come up to Mary, Joseph, and Jesus?

4. How did she respond to Jesus? How might her time at the temple have prepared her to respond this way?

Final Thought

We probably do not have the freedom that Anna had to spend all day in God's presence. But we all need to take some time each day to worship God. Only as we come to know him better are we able to recognize the great blessings that he gives us in Jesus Christ.

Pray

Our heavenly Father, we know that all good gifts come from you. And the greatest gift you have given is your one and only Son, Jesus Christ. Give us the grace to come to know you, so that we can recognize your gifts in our lives. In Jesus's name, Amen.

Sing—*What Child Is This* (p. 186)

What child is this, who, laid to rest,
On Mary's lap is sleeping?
Whom angels greet with anthems sweet,
While shepherds watch are keeping?
This, this is Christ the King,
Whom shepherds guard and angels sing;
Haste, haste to bring him laud,
The Babe, the son of Mary.

Do

Find the symbol of the praying hands. Hang this on your Jesse tree.

Further Study for Adults

Using Psalm 103, spend time in prayer praising God for his blessings in your life. Write down some specific blessings for which you are thankful.

December 21
Responses to His Coming

Only a few more days until Christmas! Have you bought all your gifts for your family members? Are the presents wrapped? Gifts are a small way that we tell others that we love them. It is hard to figure out what to give others, isn't it? Giving is the most fun when you know that the gift you have chosen is "just perfect" for the receiver. Perhaps it is a book that you know that person will cherish, a sweater in "just her color," or a piece of athletic equipment that he has his heart set on.

When Jesus was a toddler, he had some visitors who brought gifts that were "just perfect" for him. Can you guess who those visitors were? This passage begins right after Herod has instructed the Magi to go make a careful search for the child and then report back to him.

Read—*Matthew 2:9–12*

> After they had heard the king, they went on their way, and the star they had seen in the east went ahead of them until it stopped over the place where the child was. When they saw the star, they were overjoyed. On coming to the house, they saw the child with his mother Mary, and they bowed down and worshiped him. Then they opened their treasures and presented him with gifts of gold and of incense and of myrrh. And having been warned in a dream not to go back to Herod, they returned to their country by another route.

Discuss

1. When the Magi saw the star appear again, how did they feel? What did they do?
2. What did they do when they saw Jesus and his mother Mary?
3. Why do you think the Magi brought gifts to Jesus?
4. What gift can you give Jesus?

Final Thought

The gifts of the Magi each had a special meaning; each said something about who Jesus was and what he came to do. The gold, a gift for a king, showed that Jesus was truly King of kings. The incense was a gift for a priest, who burned incense in the temple as he prayed for the people. The book of Hebrews tells us that Jesus became our Great High Priest. Myrrh was a precious ointment used to prepare bodies for burial. Christ's sacrificial death for our sins was the very reason for his birth. Just as the song says, Jesus was "King, and Priest, and Sacrifice."

Pray

Dear Lord Jesus, all that I am and have, you have given to me. I cannot give a gift to you that is good enough for my King, my Great High Priest, and the One who sacrificed his life for me. All I can offer is my heart. Please take it and make it your own, for your own name's sake, Amen.

Sing—As With Gladness Men of Old (p. 189)

As they offered gifts most rare
At thy cradle rude and bare,
So may we with holy joy,
Pure and free from sin's alloy,
All our costliest treasures bring,
Christ, to thee, our heav'nly king.

Do

Place the symbol of the wise men's gifts on your Jesse tree.

Further Study for Adults

Reflect on Jesus as King, Priest, and Sacrifice. Read Hebrews 1:8–9, 4:14–16, and 10:5–10. How is Christ depicted in each of these passages? What difference does that make to you this Christmas season?

December 22
Responses to His Coming

Do you know anyone in your family or in your church who has lost a baby? We cannot understand why such things happen, and we weep many bitter tears. I hope that this has not happened in your family. If it hasn't, think of another time when you were very, very sad. Perhaps a beloved pet died, or you had to move to another town and leave a special friend. Have you ever cried so hard and felt so sad that you thought that you could never be happy again?

Remember how Herod tried to trick the Magi into telling him where Jesus was, so that he could kill the newborn king? The evil in Herod's heart made him do something that caused great sorrow.

Read—*Matthew 2:16–18*

> When Herod realized that he had been outwitted by the Magi, he was furious, and he gave orders to kill all the boys in Bethlehem and its vicinity who were two years old and under, in accordance with the time he had learned from the Magi. Then what was said through the prophet Jeremiah was fulfilled:
>> "A voice is heard in Ramah,
>> weeping and great mourning,
>> Rachel weeping for her children
>> and refusing to be comforted,
>> because they are no more."

Discuss

1. What did Herod do when the Magi did not come back and report to him where they found Jesus?
2. Who was Rachel (see Gen. 29:16–18)? She was buried near Bethlehem. All the children born in and around Bethlehem could be considered Rachel's children.

3. The prophet Jeremiah told about Rachel weeping for her children. How did that prophecy come true?
4. Why do you think Herod did such an awful thing?

Final Thought

We cannot understand why God allows such evil, cruel acts. Yet we do know that it is a part of his plan. Someday we will understand these difficult things. In fact, God tells us that in heaven, "He will wipe every tear from their eyes. There will be no more death or mourning or crying or pain, for the old order of things has passed away" (Rev. 21:4).

Pray

Almighty God and loving Father, we do not understand when we see pain and evil around us. But we believe your Word, that your purposes for us are good. We look forward to the day when you will wipe away our tears forever. In Jesus's name, Amen.

Sing—O Lord, How Shall I Meet You (p. 177)

> Love caused your incarnation;
> Love brought you down to me.
> Your thirst for my salvation
> Procured my liberty.
> Oh, love beyond all telling,
> That led you to embrace
> In love all love excelling,
> Our lost and fallen race.

Do

Find the symbol of the teardrop. Hang this on your Jesse tree.

Further Study for Adults

What sorrows and losses lie buried in your heart, a dull ache that never goes away? Write a letter to God, offering him your sorrow.

December 23
Responses to His Coming

Today and tomorrow, we will be reading exactly the same verses. But we will look at two different responses. Today we will focus in on the shepherds who came to see Jesus, and tomorrow, we will look at Mary's response.

Read—*Luke 2:15–20*

When the angels had left them and gone into heaven, the shepherds said to one another, "Let's go to Bethlehem and see this thing that has happened, which the Lord has told us about."

So they hurried off and found Mary and Joseph, and the baby, who was lying in the manger. When they had seen him, they spread the word concerning what had been told them about this child, and all who heard it were amazed at what the shepherds said to them. But Mary treasured up all these things and pondered them in her heart. The shepherds returned, glorifying and praising God for all the things they had heard and seen, which were just as they had been told.

Discuss

1. What did the shepherds say to one another when the angels left? What do you think they were feeling right then?
2. What did the shepherds do before they went to Bethlehem? (parents, this is a trick question!)
3. List all the things the shepherds did after seeing Jesus.
4. How did others respond when the shepherds told them about Jesus? Can you think of someone who might be amazed or encouraged by what the Lord has done in your life?

Final Thought

Have you ever thought about that simple phrase, "the shepherds returned"? They went back to their ordinary lives. Everything seemed just the same, back on the hillside.

But something had changed within them. They saw things differently now. They went back "glorifying and praising God." Now when they looked up at the starry sky, they remembered the angels and the wonderful message about the Savior, Christ the Lord. They remembered the baby lying in the manger, just as the angels had said. They believed that this baby would be their Savior.

When we have seen Jesus face to face, we too are changed. We see all of life with new eyes, the eyes of faith.

Pray

Dear Heavenly Father, we praise and thank you for sending a Savior, Christ the Lord. Help us to see all of life in a new way because of Jesus. In his name we pray, Amen.

Sing—*Angels We Have Heard on High* (p. 182)

Angels we have heard on high,
Sweetly singing o'er the plains,
And the mountains in reply
Echoing their joyous strains.

Gloria in excelsis Deo, Gloria in excelsis Deo.

Do

Find the symbol of the musical notes. Hang this on your Jesse tree.

Further Study for Adults

Write a prayer asking God to prepare someone's heart to receive Jesus through your words.

December 24
Responses to His Coming

Can you remember a time when something so special happened to you that you didn't want to talk about it? You just wanted to think and think, recalling every detail? For many mothers, the birth of a child is like that. It strikes us as such a miracle as we hold the precious and fragile life in our arms for the first time. In fact, the word miracle is used many times to describe it because human language cannot express what we feel at such a moment.

For Mary, Jesus's birth was more than the "ordinary miracle" of human birth. This birth was extraordinary in every way.

As you read these verses again, try to imagine what Mary was thinking and feeling.

Read—*Luke 2:15–20*

When the angels had left them and gone into heaven, the shepherds said to one another, "Let's go to Bethlehem and see this thing that has happened, which the Lord has told us about."

So they hurried off and found Mary and Joseph, and the baby, who was lying in the manger. When they had seen him, they spread the word concerning what had been told them about this child, and all who heard it were amazed at what the shepherds said to them. But Mary treasured up all these things and pondered them in her heart. The shepherds returned, glorifying and praising God for all the things they had heard and seen, which were just as they had been told.

Discuss

1. What is a treasure?
2. What do you think it means to treasure something?
3. What were the things that Mary treasured up and pondered in her heart?
4. Share some special things about Jesus that you have treasured up and pondered in your heart.

Final Thought

Are we too busy to ponder things in our hearts? If so, we are missing out on much that God wants to show us. It is my sincere prayer that these Advent devotions have helped your family take time to ponder the wonders of God's love in Jesus Christ.

Pray

Lord Jesus Christ, we worship you as King of kings and King of our hearts. We give ourselves to you. In your name, Amen.

Sing—*What Child Is This* (p. 186)

> What child is this, who, laid to rest,
> On Mary's lap is sleeping?
> Whom angels greet with anthems sweet,
> While shepherds watch are keeping?
> This, this is Christ the King,
> Whom shepherds guard and angels sing;
> Haste, haste to bring him laud,
> The Babe, the son of Mary.

Do

Find the symbol of the heart. Hang it on your Jesse tree.

Further Study for Adults

Ponder what God has shown you this Advent season.

Part 3

Celebrations

Celebrating Christmas and Epiphany

Ever since the earliest Christmas celebrations, a tension has always existed between the spiritual and "secular" aspects of the holiday. Contemporary Christians feel that tension. How should Christians observe Christmas? The Bible does not spell out the answer to this question. Church history, however, may prove helpful. Many early missionaries found deeply entrenched practices, symbols, and celebrations in the lands where they sought to spread the gospel. Rather than abolishing them, they fixed on those that were not inherently evil and applied a Christian meaning to them.

For instance, evergreens were important to the winter religious rites of the pagan tribes of Northern Europe. They signified fertility and transformation. Christian missionaries gave evergreens a new meaning. Evergreens would henceforth symbolize the everlasting life which is ours in Jesus Christ.

We, like those early Christians, find ourselves in a pagan society. Ours has been called the "post-Christian era." Vestiges of Christianity remain in our culture, but Christmas has become largely secularized. Perhaps we can take a cue from our missionary forefathers. We needn't reject the Christmas celebration out of hand, but rather allow Christ and his message to permeate our observances.

Christian families will ultimately make a difference for Christ in our society. As Jesus Christ is worshiped and celebrated in our homes, and as our homes are transformed by his love, we will become beacons of hope to our darkening world.

In the next two chapters I have included a format for family worship at Christmas, and another for celebrating Epiphany.

Family Worship at Christmas

For families with small children, a simple retelling of the narrative of Jesus's birth is quite sufficient, followed by the singing of "Away in a Manger" and "Silent Night," or other Christmas favorites. When our kids were small, we acted out Luke's story of Jesus's birth. This was always great fun. The "Family Worship at Christmas" on the following pages is best for families with children school-aged and older.

The Twelfth Night Party

January 6 is the traditional day for celebrating the close of the Christmas season. This day is called Epiphany, which means "manifestation."

Epiphany especially celebrates the visit of the Magi to Jesus, whose birth was manifested by a star. In a larger sense, Epiphany proclaims that God was manifested to the world in the person of his Son, Jesus Christ.

In earlier times, this was an important day, a festival observed by attending church services and pageants, exchanging gifts, and feasting with family and friends.

A modern-day celebration of Epiphany offers many advantages. The party can be planned and enjoyed in the relaxation of the post-Christmas season. It allows one final opportunity to sing all the favorite Christmas carols and recall all the beautiful Scriptures of Advent. Most importantly, it reiterates the spiritual significance of Christ's coming in a way that is memorable to our children.

Family Worship at Christmas

Call to Worship

Leader: "My soul glorifies the Lord and my spirit rejoices in God my Savior." (Luke 1:46, 47)

Sing—*Oh, Come, All Ye Faithful* (p. 184)

Yea, Lord, we greet thee,
Born this happy morning,
Jesus, to thee be glory given;
Word of the Father,
Now in flesh appearing:

O come, let us adore him,
O come, let us adore him,
O come, let us adore him, Christ, the Lord!

Read—*Isaiah 9:6–7*

For to us a child is born,
to us a son is given,
And the government will be on his shoulders.
And he will be called
Wonderful Counselor, Mighty God,

Everlasting Father, Prince of Peace.
Of the increase of his government and peace
there will be no end.
He will reign on David's throne
and over his kingdom,
establishing and upholding it
with justice and righteousness
from that time on and forever.
The zeal of the Lord Almighty
will accomplish this.

Sing—*Joy to the World* (p. 178)

Joy to the world! The Lord is come;
Let earth receive her King;
Let every heart prepare him room,
And heaven and nature sing.

Read—*Luke 2:1–20*

In those days Caesar Augustus issued a decree that a census
should be taken of the entire Roman world. (This was the first
census that took place while Quirinius was governor of Syria.)
And everyone went to his own town to register.

So Joseph also went up from the town of Nazareth in Galilee
to Judea, to Bethlehem the town of David, because he belonged
to the house and line of David. He went there to register with
Mary, who was pledged to be married to him and was expecting
a child. While they were there, the time came for the baby to be
born, and she gave birth to her firstborn, a son. She wrapped
him in cloths and placed him in a manger, because there was
no room for them in the inn.

And there were shepherds living out in the fields nearby,
keeping watch over their flocks at night. An angel of the Lord
appeared to them, and the glory of the Lord shone around
them, and they were terrified. But the angel said to them, "Do
not be afraid. I bring you good news of great joy that will be
for all the people. Today in the town of David a Savior has
been born to you; he is Christ the Lord. This will be a sign

to you: You will find a baby wrapped in cloths and lying in a manger."

Suddenly a great company of the heavenly host appeared with the angel, praising God and saying,

"Glory to God in the highest,
and on earth peace to men on whom his favor rests."

When the angels had left them and gone into heaven, the shepherds said to one another, "Let's go to Bethlehem and see this thing that has happened, which the Lord has told us about."

So they hurried off and found Mary and Joseph, and the baby, who was lying in the manger. When they had seen him, they spread the word concerning what had been told them about this child, and all who heard it were amazed at what the shepherds said to them. But Mary treasured up all these things and pondered them in her heart. The shepherds returned, glorifying and praising God for all the things they had heard and seen, which were just as they had been told.

Sing—*Silent Night* (p. 181)

Silent night, holy night,
All is calm, all is bright
Round yon virgin mother and child,
Holy Infant, so tender and mild,
Sleep in heavenly peace.

Silent night, holy night,
Son of God, love's pure light
Radiant beams from thy holy face,
With the dawn of redeeming grace,
Jesus, Lord, at thy birth.

Read—*Galatians 4:4–7*

But when the time had fully come, God sent his Son, born of a woman, born under law, to redeem those under law, that we might receive the full rights of sons. Because you are sons, God sent the Spirit of his Son into our hearts, the Spirit who calls out, "*Abba*, Father." So you are no longer a slave, but a son; and since you are a son, God has made you also an heir.

Discuss

1. Why did God send his Son?
2. These verses tell us that if we have accepted God's gift of his Son Jesus, we are his own children. What does it say that we call God? (*Abba* means Daddy).
3. An heir is a son who gets what belonged to his father. What belongs to God? What does God give us?

Pray

Thank you, Father, for the greatest gift of all—your Son, Our Savior, Jesus Christ the Lord.

Respond in Unison

Glory to God in the Highest, and on earth peace to men, on whom his favor rests!

Twelfth Night Party

The Twelfth Night Party is a celebration that can be enjoyed by your family alone, but it is more fun with lots of people. Invite family and friends to this festive occasion. If everyone brings a part of the meal, the burden of preparation and cost is shared.

This party consists of three elements: (1) the feast, (2) the pageant, and (3) the service.

Preparation

Invite family and friends to this Feast of Lights. If everyone brings a dish to share, the preparations are minimal.

Aside from the meal, here are the things you will need to celebrate this festival:

1. Costumes and props for the children's reenactment of the Christmas story. These can be makeshift. Let the children help assemble them.
2. Hymnbooks or song sheets with the words to all the Christmas carols.
3. Your Advent or Jesse tree, still decorated with all the symbols.
4. The Scripture references from the Advent family devotions written out on slips of paper.

The Feast

Before the festive meal is eaten, read 2 Corinthians 4:6. Briefly explain that Epiphany or the Feast of Lights celebrates God showing himself to us in the person of Jesus Christ. Offer a prayer of worship and thanksgiving.

The Pageant

As the adults are finishing the meal, the children (long since down from the table, no doubt) may don costumes and prepare to reenact the events of Christ's birth. This production can be left entirely to the children, if they are school-age. (Preschoolers will need help and prompting.) Their interpretation of the biblical account is sure to entertain the adults as well as reinforce the facts of the stories in the minds of the children.

The Service

After the pageant, it is time for the "service" of undecorating the Advent tree. Pass out hymnbooks or song sheets and the slips of paper with the verses written on them. Children too young to read verses may participate by taking symbols off the Advent or Jesse tree.

First, light candles around the room (taking every safety precaution) and offer a prayer of praise to Christ, the Light of the world. Remind everyone that tonight we celebrate the wise men following the light of the star to find the true Light of the world.

Beginning with the first symbol (the Alpha and Omega), have a child, or several children, remove each symbol from the tree, one at a time, while someone reads the corresponding verse or passage. Between the Scripture readings, sing suitable Christmas carols together. Proceed through the twenty-four days of Advent until the tree stands bare.

Conclude with a time of conversational prayer, praising and thanking God for his great gift, his Son.

Part 4

Resources

Instructions: Advent Tree Banner

For use with Advent Devotions Year One (p. 27)

The Advent tree banner is designed to enhance and reinforce the family devotions for Advent, Year One, as your family learns about Christ's coming and prepares to celebrate his birth. Each day of Advent, a symbol is added to the tree. The symbol corresponds to the Scripture reading for that day. Instructions are given for making a felt banner with felt symbols. This banner will last for years to come.

Instructions for a simpler, less permanent alternative follow on page 145.

Materials

- ⅝ yard of 36-inch-wide green felt
- ¾ yard of 36-inch-wide red or white felt
- Green thread to match felt
- Tacky glue (glue for fabrics)
- 24 adhesive-back Velcro fasteners (white circles) (Before buying these, see Other Ideas, number 2, p. 145)
- 1 dowel, ⅝-inch diameter, 26 inches long
- Felt sheets (8½ x 11) in the following colors and quantities: white (3), red (2), gold (1), blue (1), brown (1), black (1), purple (1)
- 1 length of cord, ⅛-inch diameter, 1 yard long

Instructions for Making Banner

1. Cut green felt in the shape of a Christmas tree, with the dimensions shown in Figure A.
2. Pin tree to red or white background, leaving 5 inches of background above the tree (fig. B).
3. Sew tree to red or white background, using green thread. Stitch around entire perimeter of tree (fig. B).
4. Trace and cut out the patterns on pp. 156–67.
5. Cut out the felt pieces for each of the patterns in step 4. Refer to Advent Devotions Year One to determine which symbols should be used. Check to see if color is specified in the devotion.
6. Glue the felt figures onto the appropriate felt circles. Pattern pieces indicate which color circle corresponds with each figure.
7. Apply adhesive side of hook (fuzzy) Velcro fasteners to the center of the back of each circle.
8. Apply adhesive side of loop Velcro fasteners to the Christmas tree. Space the fasteners at least 4 inches apart from each other and at least 3 inches from the edge of the banner (fig. C).
9. Fold top edge of banner over to the back side 1½ inches (fig. D).
10. Sew overlap 1 inch from fold and ½ inch from edge (fig. E). This forms the casing for the dowel.
11. Drill a hole in the dowel ¾ inch from each end (fig. F). If a drill is not available, use Option 2 in step 13.
12. Insert dowel into casing.
13. *Option 1*
    Stiffen ends of cord by wrapping with tape. Draw ends of cord through holes at ends of dowel and knot or tie cord (fig. G).
    Option 2
    Tie cord around ends of dowel. Glue cord to dowel so that cord will not slide toward center when hung (fig. H).

Other Ideas

1. Use gold braid, sequins, or other trim to decorate the tree.
2. Instead of using adhesive Velcro, you may want to get regular Velcro and sew it in place. While this is more time-consuming, it is far more durable than the adhesive-back Velcro. If you decide on this option, be sure to sew the Velcro to the back of the felt circles *before* gluing the figures to the front of the circles (step 6).
3. It is fairly easy to put the Scripture references on the back of the felt symbols. Using a ballpoint pen, write down the Scripture references for each of the Advent family devotions on iron-on laundry marking tape. Cut tape between references and affix to the back of each corresponding symbol, using the procedure indicated on the laundry tape package.

Simple Alternative to Felt Banner

If you don't have the time or the inclination to make the felt banner, use poster board and construction paper instead. Your children can color or paint the tree, decorating it with glitter, braid, etc. Then cut out and glue the symbols onto construction paper circles. Simply tape each symbol to the poster as you go through the Advent family devotions.

To Use the Advent Banner

1. Keep the felt circles (symbols) in a manila envelope or a ziplock plastic bag.
2. Before each family devotion, find the symbol indicated for that day's reading.
3. At the conclusion of each family devotion, allow a child to place the felt symbol on the tree.

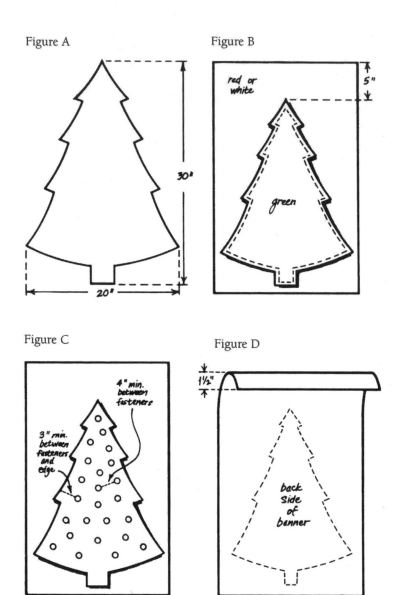

Figure A

30"

20"

Figure B

red or white

5"

green

Figure C

4" min. between fasteners

3" min. between fasteners and edge

Figure D

1½"

back side of banner

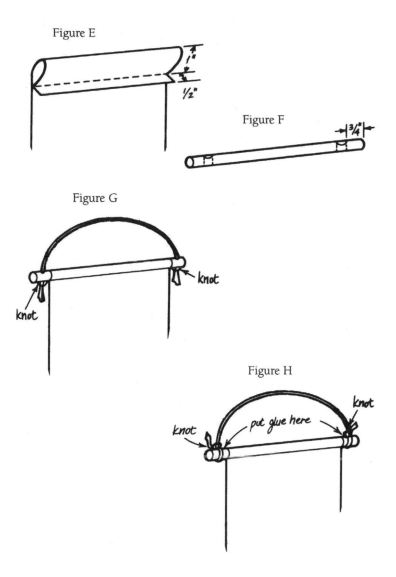

Figure E

Figure F

Figure G

knot

knot

Figure H

knot

put glue here

knot

Instructions: Jesse Tree

For use with Advent Devotions Year Two (p. 77)

The prophet Isaiah wrote: "A shoot will come up from the stump of Jesse; from his roots a Branch will bear fruit" (Isa. 11:1).

Jesus was that shoot, or branch, that grew out from the stump, or lineage, of Jesse. This prophetic image has inspired the tradition of the Jesse tree. A Jesse tree may look just like a Christmas tree, or it may look like a bare branch. What distinguishes it are its ornaments. All the ornaments have biblical significance especially pertaining to the coming of Christ.

While the idea of the Jesse tree is not original, what follows is my particular version. The symbols that are hung on the tree each evening of Advent (December 1–24) correspond to chapter 5, Advent Devotions Year Two, pages 77–129.

Jesse Tree Materials

- 1 tree branch (lightweight, but with lots of small branches)
- 1 pot or vase for holding tree branch
- Soil or rocks for weighting down pot or vase
- 1 piece of green posterboard
- Crayons or washable markers

- Scissors
- Glue or glue stick
- Paper punch
- Yarn, string, or wire ornament hooks

Instructions for Making Jesse Tree

1. Set tree branch in pot or vase. Support the tree branch by filling the vase or pot with soil or rocks. This will be the Jesse tree.
2. Photocopy the symbols for the Jesse tree on pp. 168–74.
3. The entire family can color the symbols, using crayons, markers, paints—whatever medium you choose.
4. Cut out the circles. Even small children can help as long as they have blunt-end scissors.
5. Using 1 of the circles as a pattern, draw 24 circles on the piece of green posterboard. Adults or older children will have to cut out these circles.
6. Glue the paper circles with the colored symbols onto the green posterboard circle backings. This is fun and easy for the small ones to do, especially if they have glue sticks.
7. Punch a hole in the top of each circle, about ¼ inch from the top edge.
8. Cut 24 lengths of yarn or string. Each length should be about 10 to 12 inches long. (*Option:* simply use inexpensive ornament hooks).
9. Tie strings through holes in circles. (*Option:* Put ornament hooks through holes in circles.)

To Use the Jesse Tree

1. Keep the circles (symbols) in a manila envelope or a ziplock plastic bag.
2. Before each family devotion, find the symbol indicated for that day's reading.
3. At the conclusion of each family devotion, allow a child to place the symbol on the tree.

Instructions: Advent Wreath

An Advent wreath forms an ideal centerpiece around which the family can worship. The glowing flames on the candles remind us of the star of Bethlehem. But more importantly, they remind us of the Light of the World, Jesus Christ. The lighting of the candles calls us to worship and sets this time apart as holy.

The Advent wreath consists of five candles, four around the circumference of the wreath and one in the center of the wreath. Each candle has a meaning and is lit at a particular time during Advent.

As the number of lit candles increases, so we near the celebration of Christ's coming. The ever-increasing brightness heightens our anticipation of this day.

The Significance of the Candles

The first candle to be lit, starting on the first Sunday in Advent, is the Prophecy candle. This reminds us that Christ's coming was revealed by God through the prophets hundreds of years before he was born.

The second candle is the Bethlehem candle, pointing to Christ becoming a man in Bethlehem. This is lit in addition to the first candle, starting the second Sunday in Advent.

The third candle joins the first and second on the third Sunday of Advent. This is the Shepherd's candle. With the lighting of this candle, we recognize that we, like the shepherds, must come to Christ, believe in him, and tell this good news to others.

The fourth candle, lit with the previous three beginning the fourth Sunday in Advent, is the Angel's candle. With it, we anticipate Christ's second coming and focus on his salvation.

The fifth candle, in the center of the wreath, is the Christ candle. This is lit on Christmas Day. As we light the Christ candle, we recognize that Jesus Christ, the Light of the World, is born this day.

The Significance of the Colors

Of the five candles, three are purple, one is rose, and one, white. The purple candles represent Christ's royalty. Purple also represents the attitude of humility and repentance with which we anticipate his coming. The rose candle, the Shepherd's candle, stands for God's love and faithfulness. The white candle in the center symbolizes Christ's holiness and perfection.

Evergreen Advent Wreath

Materials

- 1 round gelatin mold
- 1 block of oasis (the green foam-like material used by florists to secure cut flowers in an arrangement)
- 4 plastic candle holders for use in oasis
- 1 yard wide purple velvet ribbon (enough to go around outside of gelatin mold)
- Evergreen cuttings
- 1 set of Advent candles
- Craft glue

Instructions for Making Evergreen Advent Wreath

1. Make sure your gelatin mold is clean and dry.
2. Spread small amount of craft glue in 1½-inch band around outer side of gelatin mold. Glue velvet ribbon here. Allow glue to dry.
3. Cut your oasis into cubes just a bit larger than your gelatin mold is wide.
4. Squeeze oasis cubes into gelatin mold until the mold has enough oasis to hold candle holders and plenty of evergreen cuttings, but there is still room for some water (to keep the evergreens fresh).
5. Insert plastic candle holders into oasis, spacing then evenly.
6. Insert evergreen cuttings into oasis. Fill gelatin mold with water. Refill periodically throughout the month to ensure that evergreens stay fresh and do not present fire hazard.
7. Put Advent candles into candle holders.
8. Be sure to protect furniture from water that may spill when table is bumped.

Pie Plate Advent Wreath

Purchase a 9-inch aluminum pie plate. Turn it upside down and carefully cut Xs in the appropriate locations. Insert the bases of the candles in the Xs. Decorate the pie plate with greens.

Freestanding Advent Wreath

Use five small free-standing candle holders. Place four around the outside of a decorated grapevine or styrofoam wreath. Place the fifth candle holder (for the white Christ candle) in the center of the wreath.

Store-Bought Advent Wreath

Purchase an Advent wreath at a local Christian bookstore. (These are readily available and inexpensive.) Purchase a thicker white candle that can be set in a holder or on a saucer in the center. Decorate the wreath with additional fresh or artificial greens, if desired.

To Use the Advent Wreath

Light the appropriate candle(s) at the beginning of each family time. (A parent should do this, for safety reasons.) Each time a new candle is lit (each Sunday during Advent), read and discuss the meaning of that new candle.

At the conclusion of each family time, extinguish the candles. Children may take turns blowing out the candles. Caution should be used at all times. Note: protect furniture from candle wax. My experience has been that Advent candles drip quite a bit (aided by lots of blowing, no doubt!).

12

Symbol Patterns

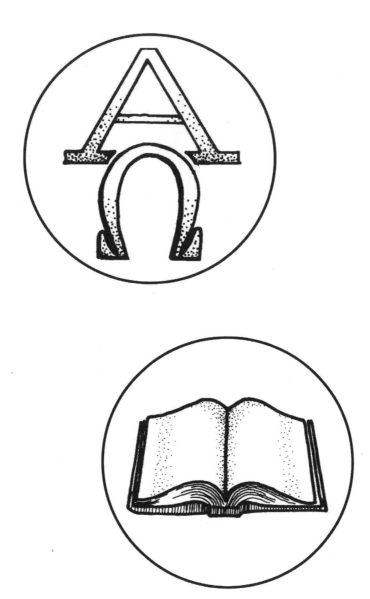

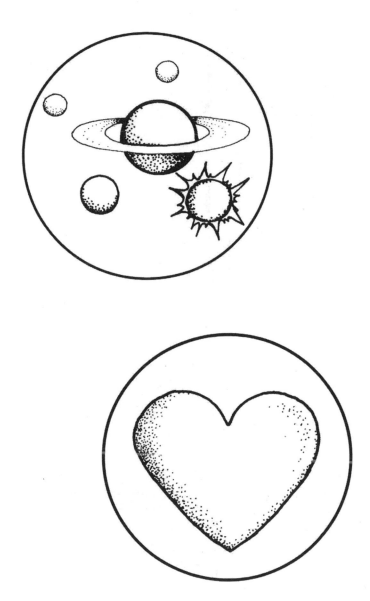

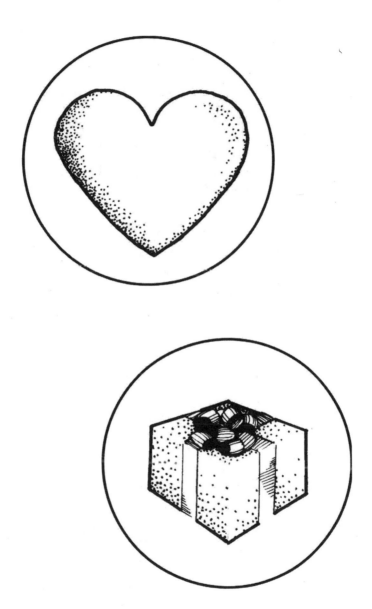

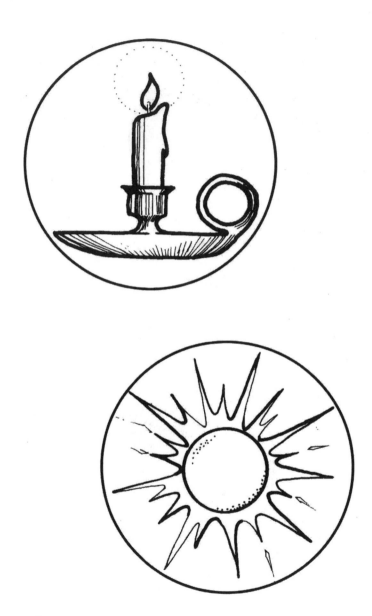

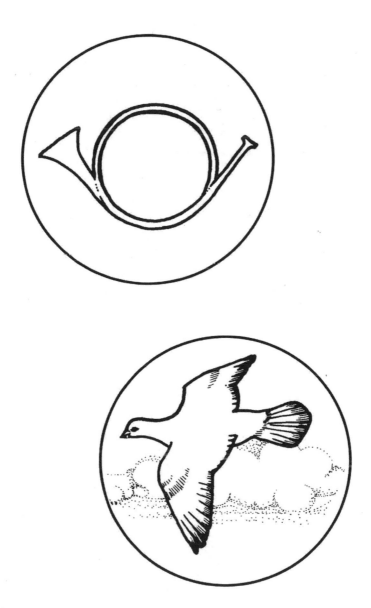

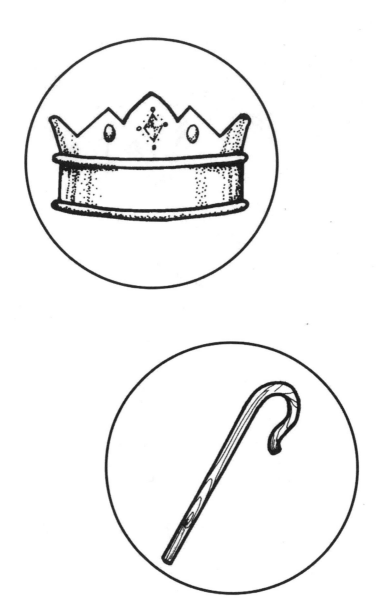

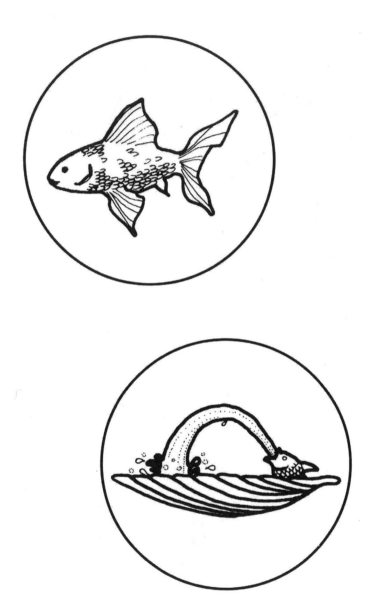

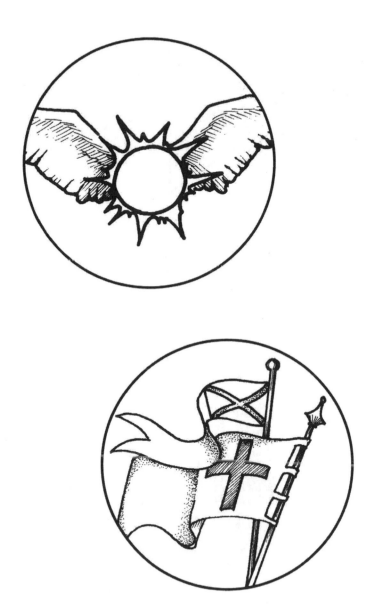

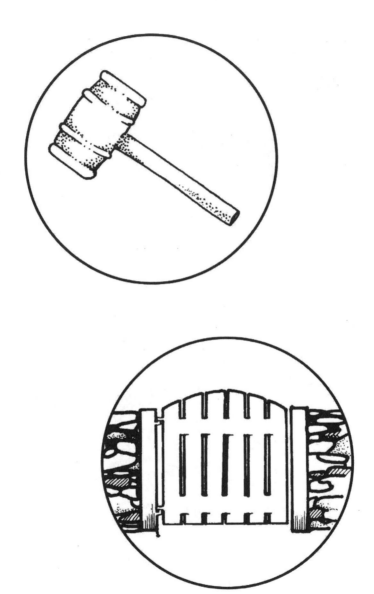

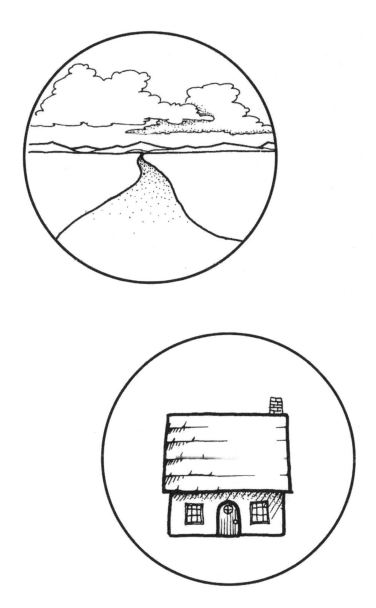

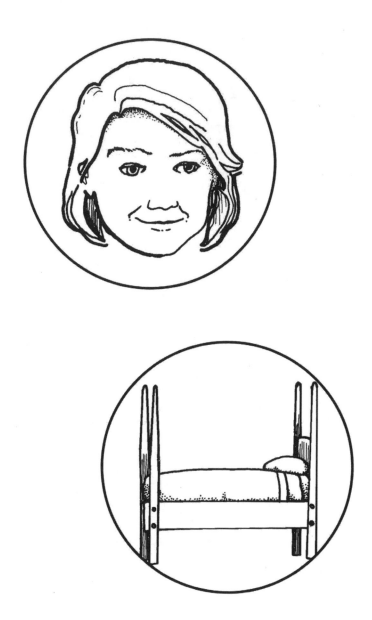

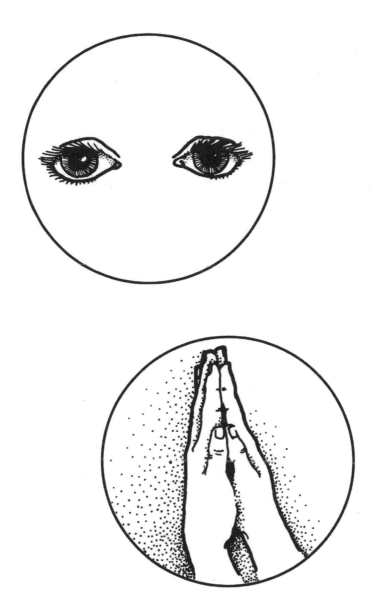

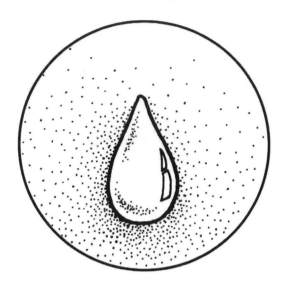

Hymns

Oh, Come, Oh, Come, Emmanuel

1 Oh, come, oh, come, Em - man - u - el, And ran - som cap - tive
2 Oh, come, oh, come, great Lord of might, Who to your tribes on
3 Oh, come, strong Branch of Jes - se, free Your own from Sa - tan's
4 Oh, come, blest Day-spring, come and cheer Our spir - its by your

Is - ra - el, That mourns in lone - ly ex - ile here
Si - nai's height In an - cient times once gave the law
tyr - an - ny; From depths of hell your peo - ple save
ad - vent here; Dis - perse the gloom - y clouds of night,

Un - til the Son of God ap - pear.
In cloud, and maj - es - ty, and awe.
And give them vic - t'ry o'er the grave.   *Refrain* Re-joice! Re-joice!
And death's dark shad - ows put to flight.

Em - man - u - el Shall come to you, O Is - ra - el.

O Lord, How Shall I Meet You

1 O Lord, how shall I meet you, How wel-come you a-right? Your peo-ple long to greet you, My hope, my heart's de-light! Oh, kin-dle, Lord most ho-ly, Your lamp with-in my breast To do in spir-it low-ly All that may please you best.

2 Your Zi-on strews be-fore you Green boughs and fair-est palms; And I, too, will a-dore you With joy-ous songs and psalms. My heart shall bloom for-ev-er For you with prais-es new And from your name shall nev-er With-hold the hon-or due.

3 I lay in fet-ters, groan-ing; You came to set me free. I stood, my shame be-moan-ing; You came to hon-or me, A glo-rious crown you give me, A trea-sure safe on high That will not fail or leave me As earth-ly rich-es fly.

4 Love caused your in-car-na-tion; Love brought you down to me. Your thirst for my sal-va-tion Pro-cured my lib-er-ty. Oh, love be-yond all tell-ing, That led you to em-brace In love, all love ex-cel-ling, Our lost and fall-en race.

Joy to the World

O Little Town of Bethlehem

1 O lit - tle town of Beth - le - hem, How still we see thee lie!
2 For Christ is born of Mar - y, And, gath - ered all a - bove
3 How si - lent - ly, how si - lent - ly The won - drous gift is giv'n!
4 O ho - ly Child of Beth - le - hem, De - scend to us, we pray;

A - bove thy deep and dream-less sleep The si - lent stars go by;
While mor - tals sleep, the an - gels keep Their watch of won-d'ring love.
So God im - parts to hu - man hearts The bless - ings of his heav'n.
Cast out our sin, and en - ter in, Be born in us to - day.

Yet in thy dark streets shin - eth The ev - er - last - ing light.
O morn - ing stars, to - geth - er Pro - claim the ho - ly birth,
No ear may hear his com - ing: But, in this world of sin,
We hear the Christ - mas an - gels The great glad tid - ings tell;

The hopes and fears of all the years Are met in thee to - night.
And prais - es sing to God the king, And peace to all the earth!
Where meek souls will re - ceive him, still The dear Christ en - ters in.
Oh, come to us, a - bide with us, Our Lord Im - man - u - el!

Hark! The Herald Angels Sing

1 Hark! The her - ald an - gels sing, "Glo - ry to the new - born king;
2 Christ, by high - est heav'n a - dored, Christ, the ev - er - last - ing Lord,
3 Hail the heav'n - born Prince of Peace! Hail the sun of right - teous - ness!

Peace on earth, and mer - cy mild, God and sin - ners rec - on - ciled."
Late in time be - hold him come, Off - spring of a vir - gin's womb.
Light and life to all he brings, Ris'n with heal - ing in his wings.

Joy - ful, all you na - tions, rise; Join the tri - umph of the skies;
Veiled in flesh the God - head see! Hail, in - car - nate de - i - ty!
Mild he lays his glo - ry by, Born that we no more may die,

With an - gel - ic hosts pro - claim, "Christ is born in Beth - le - hem!"
Pleased as man with us to dwell, Je - sus, our Em - man - u - el!
Born to raise each child of earth, Born to give us sec - ond birth.

Hark! The her - ald an - gels sing, "Glo - ry to the new - born king!"

Silent Night

1 Si - lent night, ho - ly night! All is calm, all is bright Round yon
2 Si - lent night, ho - ly night! Shep-herds quake at the sight; Glo - ries
3 Si - lent night, ho - ly night! Son of God, love's pure light Ra - diant

vir - gin moth - er and child. Ho - ly In - fant, so ten - der and mild,
stream from heav - en a - far, Heav'n - ly hosts . . . sing, Al - le - lu - ia!
beams from your ho - ly face, With the dawn of re - deem - ing grace,

Sleep in heav - en - ly peace, Sleep in heav - en - ly peace.
Christ, the Sav - ior, is born! Christ, the Sav - ior, is born!
Je - sus, Lord, at your birth, Je - sus, Lord, at your birth.

Angels We Have Heard on High

Good Christian Friends Rejoice

1 Good Chris-tian friends, re - joice
2 Good Chris-tian friends, re - joice
3 Good Chris-tian friends, re - joice

With heart and soul and voice;
With heart and soul and voice;
With heart and soul and voice;

Give ye heed to what we say:
Now ye hear of end - less bliss:
Now ye need not fear the grave;

Je - sus Christ is born to - day;
Je - sus Christ was born for this!
Je - sus Christ was born to save!

Ox and ass be - fore him bow, And he is in the man - ger now.
He has o - pened heav - en's door, And we are blest for - ev - er - more.
Calls you one and calls you all To gain his ev - er - last - ing hall.

Christ is born to - day!
Christ was born for this!
Christ was born to save!

Christ is born to - day!
Christ was born for this!
Christ was born to save!

Oh, Come, All Ye Faithful

1 Oh, come, all ye faith - ful, Joy - ful and tri - um - phant! Oh,
2 The high - est, most ho - ly, Light of light e - ter - nal,
3 Sing, choirs of an - gels, Sing in ex - ul - ta - tion,
4 Yea, Lord, we greet thee, Born this hap - py morn - ing;

come ye, oh, come . . ye to Beth - le - hem;
Born of a vir - gin, a mor - tal he comes;
Sing, all ye cit - i - zens of heav - en a - bove!
Je - sus, to thee . . be . . glo - ry giv'n!

Come and be - hold him Born the king of an - gels:
Son of the Fa - ther Now in flesh ap - pear - ing!
Glo - ry to God . . . . In . . . the . . high - est:
Word of the Fa - ther, Now in flesh ap - pear - ing:

Refrain

Oh, come, let us a - dore him, Oh, come, let us a - dore him,

Oh, come, let us a - dore him, Christ the Lord!

Once Again My Heart Rejoices

1 Once a - gain my heart re - joic - es As I hear, far and near,
2 Hark! A voice from yon - der man - ger, Soft and sweet, does en - treat,
3 Come, then, let us has - ten yon - der; Here let all, great and small,

Sweet-est an - gel voic - es; "Christ is born,"their choirs are sing - ing,
"Flee from woe and dan - ger; Come and see; from all that grieves you
Kneel in awe and won - der; Love him who with love is yearn - ing;

Till the air ev - 'ry - where Now with joy is ring - ing.
You are freed; all you need I will sure - ly give you."
Hail the star that from far Bright with hope is burn - ing.

What Child Is This

All Glory, Laud, and Honor

Refrain

All glo - ry, laud, and hon - or To you, re - deem - er, king,

To whom the lips of chil - dren Made sweet ho - san - nas ring.

1. You are the king of Is - rael And Da - vid's roy - al Son.
2. The com - pa - ny of an - gels Are prais - ing you on high;
3. The mul - ti - tude of pil - grims With palms be - fore you went.
4. To you, be - fore your Pas - sion, They sang their hymns of praise.

Refrain

Now in the Lord's name com - ing, Our King and Bless - ed One.
Cre - a - tion and all mor - tals In cho - rus make re - ply.
Our praise and prayer and an - thems Be - fore you we pre - sent.
To you, now high ex - alt - ed, Our mel - o - dy we raise.

Away in a Manger

1 A - way   in   a   man - ger, no   crib   for   his   bed,   The   lit - tle Lord
2 The cat - tle   are   low - ing; the   poor   ba - by wakes,   But   lit - tle Lord
3 Be near   me, Lord   Je - sus;   I   ask   you   to   stay   Close by   me for -

Je - sus   laid   down   his   sweet head;   The   stars   in   the   sky . . looked
Je - sus   no   cry - ing   he makes.   I   love   you, Lord   Je - sus;   look
ev - er   and   love   me,   I   pray.   Bless   all   the   dear   chil - dren   in

down where he   lay,   The   lit - tle Lord   Je - sus   a - sleep   on   the   hay.
down from the   sky   And stay   by   my   cra - dle   till   morn - ing   is   nigh.
your   ten - der   care   And   fit   us   for   heav - en   to   live   with you   there.

As With Gladness Men of Old

1 As with glad-ness men of old Did the guid-ing star be-hold;
2 As with joy-ful steps they sped, Sav-ior, to thy low-ly bed,
3 As they of-fered gifts most rare At thy cra-dle, rude and bare,
4 Ho-ly Je-sus, ev-'ry day Keep us in the nar-row way;

As with joy they hailed its light, Lead-ing on-ward, beam-ing bright;
There to bend the knee be-fore Thee, whom heav'n and earth a-dore;
So may we with ho-ly joy, Pure and free from sin's al-loy,
And when earth-ly things are past, Bring our ran-somed souls at last

So, most gra-cious Lord, may we Ev-er-more be led by thee.
So may we with will-ing feet Ev-er seek thy mer-cy seat.
All our cost-liest trea-sures bring, Christ, to thee, our heav'n-ly king.
Where they need no star to guide, Where no clouds thy glo-ry hide.

Angels from the Realms of Glory

1 An - gels, from the realms of glo - ry, Wing your flight o'er all the earth;
2 Shep-herds, in the fields a - bid - ing, Watch-ing o'er your flocks by night,
3 Sa - ges, leave your con - tem-pla-tions, Bright - er vi - sions beam a - far;
4 All cre - a - tion, join in prais-ing God, the Fa - ther, Spir - it, Son,

Once you sang cre - a - tion's sto - ry; Now pro-claim Mes - si - ah's birth:
God with us is now re - sid - ing, Yon - der shines the in - fant light.
Seek the great de - sire of na - tions, You have seen his na - tal star.
Ev - er-more your voic - es rais - ing To the e - ter - nal Three in One.

Refrain

Come and wor - ship, come and wor - ship, Wor - ship Christ, the new - born king.

190